In Search

OF THE

Shroud of Turin

In Search

OF THE

Shroud of Turin

New Light on Its History and Origins

ROBERT DREWS

Atheist
Humanist

Rowman & Allanheld
PUBLISHERS

ROWMAN & ALLANHELD

Published in the United States of America in 1984
by Rowman & Allanheld, Publishers
(A division of Littlefield, Adams & Company)
81 Adams Drive, Totowa, New Jersey 07512

Library of Congress Cataloging in Publication Data

Drews, Robert.
  In search of the Shroud of Turin.

  Bibliography: p.
  Includes index.
  1. Holy shroud. I. Title.
BT587.S4D7 1984   232.9′66   83-24586
ISBN 0-8476-7349-9

    85   86 / 10 9 8 7 6 5 4 3 2
Printed in the United States of America

Contents

Illustrations

Plates

Acknowledgments

In the making of this book I have needed and received assistance from many people. Professors Arthur Dewey, William Race and Daniel Scavone read the manuscript critically and provided me with many useful suggestions. These scholars, of course, not only bear no responsibility for the argument of the book, but even (in varying degrees) are in complete disagreement with some of its conclusions. I am most grateful for their criticism, negative as well as positive.

In a less formal way, I have been much helped by those who took the time to listen and object to my arguments in a primitive stage. For almost a year and a half my wife, Phoebe, added the role of critic to all her other roles; without complaint she heard far more about the Shroud than she could have wished, and gave much good advice. My former colleague, Professor Gerd Luedemann, gently but firmly steered me away from some of my early and ill-conceived speculation about the growth of several New Testament traditions. Professor Ljubica Popovich patiently answered my questions about early Christian and Byzantine art. Other colleagues and students, among whom I must mention especially Mr. Randy Todd, have given freely of their time and good judgment.

I am also grateful to specialists on the Shroud who assisted me. Conversations with Professor Scavone, whose familiarity with current Shroud research is extraordinary, were as pleasant as they were profitable. Father Adam J. Otterbein, president of the Holy Shroud Guild, generously provided me with materials and information. Father Francis Filas, of Loyola University in Chicago, made available to me the full report of his findings.

And Mr. Frank Tribbe, author of a recent book on the Shroud, gave me timely advice. These specialists' beliefs about the Shroud differ significantly from my own, and I therefore appreciate their cooperation all the more.

For typing the manuscript from a draft that was often almost illegible, and for correcting infelicities along the way, I am grateful to Mrs. Sonny Wiesmeyer. I am indebted to two persons whom I have not met at the publishing offices of Rowman & Allanheld: Ms. Tobi Krutt, who skillfully handled the problems of production, and Ms. Janet S. Johnston, who edited the manuscript with a rare combination of discretion and high standards.

The securing of photographs and of permission to publish them is a complex process, and I thank those who made things easier. For the Holy Shroud Guild, Father Otterbein provided illustrations of the Shroud free of charge; Plates 1–4 are here published through the courtesy of the Holy Shroud Guild. Ms. Karin Einaudi, who presides so efficiently over the Fototeca Unione at the American Academy in Rome, helped me to obtain the photographs for Plates 5–8; they are published with the permission of the Pontificia Commissione di Archeologia Sacra in Rome. Plate 9 is published with the permission of Art Resource, in New York. Professor André Grabar, dean of historians of early Christian art, promptly and cordially gave me permission to reproduce material from his *La Sainte Face de Laon* (Prague, Seminarium Kondakovianum, 1931); Plates 10 and 11 are taken from that book.

Finally and especially, I owe much to Mr. Spencer Carr, editor at Rowman & Allanheld. He read the manuscript, liked it, suggested improvements, worked for its acceptance for publication, and has given indispensable assistance in many other ways. Without his help, this book would still be a manuscript in my desk drawer.

Note: Translations of New Testament passages are taken from the Authorized (King James) Version; translations of other Greek or Latin texts, unless otherwise noted, are my own.

Introduction

ON the Shroud of Turin is a dim but unmistakable image of a man whose face resembles the face of Jesus conventional in Christian art, and whose body exhibits what seem to be the wounds of crucifixion. In the last few years the Shroud, acclaimed as the burial shroud of Jesus Christ, has begun to catch the world's attention. Television programs, a film, books, magazine and newspaper articles have made the Shroud a subject of conversation for millions who until recently had known nothing about it. Many intelligent men and women, knowing the public's endless fascination with the bizarre and the fantastic, regard this swelling interest with contempt. Such a reaction is understandable but regrettable.

It is not a surprise that much is being written about the Shroud. The 1978 exhibit of the Shroud was sure to generate interest in the relic, just as an exhibit in 1898 inspired a dozen books. This time, however, the interest is more than a meteoric fad. For the last twenty years public opinion has been slowly shifting in favor of the Shroud, mostly because a few scientists have provided a respectable argument that it is an ancient cloth, and that the image it carries may very well be Jesus' image. The Shroud is still ignored or dismissed by most academicians, but partisans who have followed its recent career sense that even in the academy the Shroud's day is about to dawn.

Despite all that has recently been written about the Shroud (half a dozen books on the subject have been published this last year in America alone), there are still available only two explanations, both of them well worn, of what the Shroud is. One recent book maintains, as did most informed people at one time, that the Shroud is a fourteenth-century forgery. The other new books on the Shroud all conclude that the cloth did indeed cover Jesus' body in the tomb, and they either imply or suggest outright that the image was miraculously wrought, probably at the moment of Jesus' resurrection. It is frequently supposed that these two are the only possible explanations of the Shroud: either it is the miraculously imprinted burial shroud of Jesus, or it is a medieval forgery.

These may not, however, be the only—or even the most likely—explanations of the Shroud. There is much more to be said about the Shroud—in fact, so much more that serious discussion of the subject seems still to be at a fairly preliminary stage. Specifically, while science has been brought to bear on the Shroud, history has not, and the light that history can shed upon the matter is indispensable for an intelligent judgment of what the Shroud may or may not be. It is conceivable, for example, that the Shroud does carry the direct image of Jesus' body, but that the image was not effected miraculously. On the other hand, it is also conceivable that the image was forged, not in the fourteenth century, but early in Christian antiquity.

It is in this middle ground that the present study finds an explanation of the Shroud: its mysterious image is neither a medieval forgery nor a miraculous imprint of Jesus' body. In the canonical and apocryphal books of the New Testament, in the writings of the early Church Fathers and of Byzantine and Syriac authors, and in the representations of Jesus in early Christian art are hidden the clues to the Shroud's history and origins.

If the Shroud's history as reconstructed here is correct, the implications are enormous. The Shroud in that case provides critical testimony on the early Christian Church, on the traditions about Jesus' teachings, and on the historicity of his physical resurrection. The Shroud is supposed, by many contemporary Christians, to support the belief in Jesus' bodily resurrection. And it is especially for that reason that the Shroud deserves to be studied, with meticulous patience and uncompromising objectivity. The stakes are too high for us to do otherwise.

The conclusions reached in this book will probably be as unexpected for most readers as they were for me. Although from time to time I had heard of the Shroud, my interest in it was finally awakened by a popular article, Cullen Murphy's "Shreds of Evidence," in the November 1981 issue of *Harper's*. This article, illustrated with the famous and fascinating photographs, persuaded me that here was something extraordinary. During my subsequent study of the Shroud's history my understanding of this amazing object changed radically, for the secret of the Shroud is revealed in its history. The conclusions presented here seem to me clearly indicated by the evidence. Whether they will stand up under critical scrutiny is for others to decide.

i / Historians and the Shroud

THE Shroud of Turin has an eccentric following. At one and the same time the Shroud has been the object of enormous interest and thoroughly ignored. It is an artifact so precious that three centuries ago a cathedral chapel was constructed specifically to house and protect it, and so famous that at its most recent public display in the autumn of 1978, more than three million people came to view it. We may safely say that no single object is as venerated by the Christian world as is the Shroud of Turin.

But the Shroud has scarcely been noticed by those who, one would suppose, should have a professional interest in it: scholars whose province includes the ancient world and the beginnings of Christianity. An index of this massive indifference is the absence of the Shroud from the professional literature of church historians, archaeologists, New Testament scholars, ancient historians, and Classicists (all of whom I shall for convenience lump together under the single heading "historians"). Consider, for example, the annual bibliography *L'Année philologique*, which presents what is assumed to be an exhaustive list of all books and articles relevant to the Greco-Roman world. Among the approximately 10,000 titles that appear in any given year, one will not find in *L'Année philologique* Pietro Savio's scholarly study on the Shroud, published in 1957, nor Ian Wilson's *The Shroud of Turin*, which appeared in 1978,[1] nor any other book whose subject is the Shroud. Nor, with an occasional exception, will one find publications about the Shroud in the bibliographies of New Testament studies or Biblical archaeology.[2] The reason for this indifference, of course, has been the assumption (almost universal among historians) that the Shroud is a fake. Only if it were demonstrated that the Shroud is not a fake would historians be obliged to deal with it and its implications.

Fortunately, what professional historians have neglected has been studied intensely by others, and a varied and colorful company has produced a considerable literature about the Shroud. These somewhat clandestine articles tend to appear in obscure journals, and what books there are on the subject have not been published by university presses. Among those who have contributed to present knowledge of (or theories about) the Shroud are physicians, chemists, photographers, journalists, physicists, a coroner, a criminologist, and even a stage magician. To them, and not to professional historians, credit must be given both for insisting upon the profound importance of the Shroud, and for launching an investigation of its nature and authenticity.[3]

That the scholarly world has been so reluctant to turn its attention to the Shroud may at first glance seem puzzling, but is explicable all the same. The Shroud is a sheet of linen bearing frontal and dorsal images of a body said to be the crucified body of Jesus Christ. This sensational, or even preposterous, claim is itself an explanation for the indifference of scholarly historians: an object touted as a memento from the crucifixion of Jesus, and so from the central episode in Western history, is obviously too good to be true. So many relics of Jesus' passion—fragments of the cross, drops of the holy blood, the crown of thorns—were "discovered" in the Middle Ages, only to be derided in the Enlightenment, that by the nineteenth century an historian who maintained the authenticity of a relic was invariably looked at askance by his colleagues, and was in some danger of losing his standing altogether in the scholarly community. This instinctive wariness of nineteenth-century historians toward Christian relics was in the case of the Shroud aggravated by two special circumstances. First was an insidious presupposition: the Shroud attests to the Resurrection of Jesus; but resurrection of a dead body is impossible; therefore the Shroud must be a hoax. Second, the Shroud was virtually inaccessible in the nineteenth century. Exhibitions were few and far between: many of the pilgrims who saw the Shroud at its 1898 exposition had not yet been born when it had last been exhibited in 1868. And what one knew of the Shroud came from hearsay. There were no photographs of the Shroud; such paintings as existed were much influenced by imagination and certainly provided no basis for study. And so it happened that when, in the nineteenth century, the foundations of scholarly history were being laid, historians could not have dreamt that one day they might be taken to task for not including the Shroud in their foundations.

A ripple of interest occurred in 1898 when an amateur photographer, Secondo Pia, was invited to make photographs of the Shroud as part of the exposition activities. One of the most dramatic moments in the Shroud's history came when Pia examined the negatives he had obtained: instead of a normal negative image, with light and shade reversed, of the faint figure on the Shroud, Pia saw a *positive* image in which the features of the "Man of the Shroud" were for the first time clearly and sharply revealed. In other words, the Shroud was itself something of a photographic negative. Newspapers around the world announced Pia's exciting discovery, and the reading public was tantalized by the mysterious—or even miraculous—nature of the Shroud's image. Scholars were also forced to take notice. It is ironic that in 1898 Ernst von Dobschuetz was putting the finishing touches on his magnificent *Christusbilder*, which remains the definitive scholarly description and analysis of all the purportedly sacred pictures of Jesus. Although von Dobschuetz had all but completed his work before the exposition at Turin yielded Pia's amazing negatives, he mentions them briefly in a footnote.[4]

All in all, the impact of Pia's negatives was neither as stunning nor as enduring as one might suppose. The technology for reproducing photographs in newspapers was still too primitive to convey exactly what Pia had discovered. More important, the sudden attention to the Shroud, generated by both the exposition and the photographs, almost immediately provoked the first scholarly examination of the Shroud's credentials. In 1899 a noted French Catholic scholar, Abbé Ulysse Chevalier, began reporting his findings, and they were devastating.[5] Chevalier had never seen the Shroud, or even good reproductions of Pia's photographs, but he knew his way around the documents of medieval history better than anyone else. A fourteenth-century bishop, Chevalier discovered, had declared the Shroud a forgery when it was first displayed, and had even obtained a confession from the man who had painted the image. Thus Chevalier demonstrated to the satisfaction of most historians that the Shroud, like so many other famous relics, was a medieval hoax.

While historians were deciding against it, several scientists threw their considerable weight in favor of the Shroud's authenticity. Secondo Pia sent a set of photographs—both positive and negative—on glass plates to the Sorbonne, and a group of young scientists there were quickly convinced that the images on the Shroud could not have been painted. The leading spirit among the young scientists was an instructor in biology, Paul Vignon, who was to spend the rest of his life defending the Shroud's credentials. Neither Vignon nor his associates, however, had a reputation to stake on the matter, and Parisian society did not pay much attention to their pronouncements until the group won over a widely respected figure: Yves Delage, who at the turn of the century was the Sorbonne's distinguished professor of comparative anatomy. It is ironic that Delage, who was a religious agnostic (and continued to be an agnostic during and after his study of the Shroud) was thus cast as the champion of the Shroud's authenticity, while the Abbot Ulysse Chevalier led a phalanx of Catholic historians who declared the Shroud a fraud. Delage insisted that the anatomical detail revealed by Pia's photographs was too correct to have been produced by an artist, and Delage also observed a complete correspondence between the apparent wounds and the apparent physical abnormalities of the Man of the Shroud (for example, no thumbs are visible on the hands of the Man of the Shroud: a nail through the wrist at the point of the bloodstain would have caused the thumb to retract). On April 21, 1902 in a tumultuous session of the French Academy, Delage presented his conclusion: anatomical considerations indicated that the Shroud had indeed been imprinted by the body of a man who had been crucified. Delage was convinced that man was Jesus. Together with Vignon and other colleagues in the field of medicine, Delage proposed an explanation of how the image might have been formed: it was probably the result of vapors produced by the combination of burial ointments (aloes in particular) and the urea-laden sweat secreted during severe torture. The Shroud, in other words, presented a remarkable, though not a miraculous, "vaporograph" of the body of Jesus Christ.

Many members of the French Academy found Delage's conclusions incredible. Even though Delage had not postulated a miracle, the Academicians reasoned that a "vaporograph" such as the one Delage described would have been nothing less than a miracle, no matter how clinically Delage and his associates had explained the mechanism of its formation. Not being inclined to accept miracles, the Academicians decided that Delage must be wrong and that the Abbé Chevalier must be right: the Shroud's image had been forged by a fourteenth-century artist.

And so the argument seemed headed for resolution, not only in France but throughout Europe. Many years later Father Edward A. Wuenschel, a long-time stalwart of the Holy Shroud Guild, looked back on this turn-of-the-century debate and wrote some sour words about the damage done to the Shroud's reputation by "documents exhumed from the dust of archives and libraries." The fresh and objective arguments of science had been rejected in favor of a libelous fourteenth-century text. "The learned dons, fascinated by those precious documents, solemnly awarded the verdict to the opposition. Every encyclopedia and reference work dutifully registered the verdict and consigned the Shroud to the limbo of spurious relics. Chevalier had triumphed over Vignon and Delage."[6] In the English-speaking world the spurious origin of the Shroud was forcefully argued by a Jesuit, Father Herbert Thurston, in a series of articles beginning in 1903.[7] Since Thurston's articles appeared in *The Month*, widely distributed among the Catholic laity, and in the *Catholic Encyclopedia* (Thurston's entry there was not replaced until 1968), much of the general reading public joined the scholarly community in dismissing the Shroud.

A contributing factor to the failure of Vignon's and Delage's thesis was the inability of scientists to duplicate the "vaporograph" that the thesis required. Vignon conducted several experiments which, in his opinion, showed that a mixture of ammonia and aloes does release an image-producing vapor. Other observers, however, found the experimental images disappointing, and they concluded that vapors rising even a short distance can produce at best an image far more blurred and diffuse than that of the Shroud.

In the academic arena, Chevalier and Thurston did not win their battle without the considerable, though unintended, aid of Ernst von Dobschuetz. Any historian who, on the basis of Pia's photographs and Delage's arguments, may have been tempted to take the Shroud seriously would no longer have been so inclined after confronting the impeccable scholarship of von Dobschuetz's *Christusbilder*.[8] Von Dobschuetz pointed out that the notion of divinely wrought images began with the ancient Greeks (the best known of their images being the Palladion, an image of Athena sent down to mankind from Mt. Olympus), and he presented, in their original languages or in German translation, more than fifteen centuries' accumulation of stories about sacred images of Jesus. Here were included accounts of the several miraculous cloths on which Jesus had impressed his face, the most notorious being the Veronica veil and the Mandylion, which for centuries prior to its disappearance had been the most sacred relic in Constantinople; here were other representations of the Savior that were "not made by human hands"; here, too, were portraits of Jesus painted by Mary, by Peter and Paul, and especially by Luke. These images not only had a wondrous origin, but through the centuries had worked a great variety of miracles for the individuals, churches, or cities whose property they were. When one looks over the hundreds of texts that von Dobschuetz transcribed from the Greek, Latin, Syriac, and other languages, one cannot escape the conclusion that the Christians of antiquity and the Middle Ages were capable of believing—so great was their credulity and ignorance—almost anything that resourceful minds could invent.

It is no surprise, then, that historians in the twentieth century, like their nineteenth-century predecessors, have for the most part taken for granted that the Shroud is merely one of many products of pious ingenuity. What von Dobschuetz concluded about the entire gallery of Jesus-portraits, and what Chevalier discovered about the Shroud in particular, convinced historians that there was not even a remote possibility that the Shroud bore the image of Jesus' body. The verdict of historians shaped scholarly opinion on the matter for more than two generations.

An indication of what educated persons thought—or were supposed to think—about the Shroud is the fact that the *Encyclopedia Britannica* did not even include an entry on the Shroud until the 1960s.

Yet belief remained. Especially in Catholic Europe, millions of twentieth-century Christians, unaffected by the historians' conclusions, believed the Shroud is genuine. The photographs, more than anything else, encouraged the belief. They showed a face remarkably similar to the conventional face of Jesus in Christian art, and a body whose wounds corresponded exactly to the Gospels' account of his passion. In 1931 the Shroud was photographed again, this time by a professional photographer, Giuseppe Enrie, with a camera considerably more sophisticated than that used by Pia, and the results were even more gratifying. The photographs led to the formation of societies for the publicizing and veneration of the Shroud, and people from various walks of life became spare-time sindonologists (*sindon* is the Greek work for the "linen sheet" in which, the Gospels say, Joseph of Arimathea wrapped the body of Jesus after taking it down from the cross). Paul Vignon, who remained a sindonologist until his death, made an exhaustive study of the similarities between the face of the Man of the Shroud and the face of Christ in medieval, Byzantine, and Renaissance art.[9] A French physician, Pierre Barbet, studied the apparent bloodstains on the arms of the Man of the Shroud and in macabre detail explained how they testified to death on a cross.[10]

The enthusiasm and industry of individual sindonologists eventually set larger forces in motion. Except during expositions, the Shroud has for more than four centuries rested securely, hidden from view, in the huge Cathedral of San Giovanni Battista in Turin. No matter how high their rank or noble their purpose, visitors to the cathedral can see only the ornate casket, protected by a grille, in which the Shroud reposes. What sindonologists were able to deduce, therefore, came not from first-hand observation of the Shroud, but from the photographs taken by Pia and Enrie. By the 1960s, confidence in the authenticity of the Shroud was deep enough and widespread enough that Cardinal Pellegrino, Archbishop of Turin, decided it was time the Shroud be submitted to scientific examination.[11] Permission for such an examination was obtained from Umberto, the exiled king of Italy and the nominal owner of the Shroud, and in 1969 the Cardinal appointed a panel of experts to prepare an agenda of appropriate tests. The commission of eleven men and one woman was, by parochial standards, distinguished. In addition to three priests, the panel included two of northern Italy's most respected professors of forensic medicine, the director of a radiological laboratory in one of Turin's major hospitals, the curator of Turin's Egyptian museum, and other prominent academics from the Italian Piedmont and the Po valley. The climax of years of preparation and anticipation came on November 22 through 24, 1973. After a private showing to invited guests, the Shroud was exhibited and discussed on television, before an audience of millions spread over much of Europe. On November 24th, threads were taken from the Shroud for analysis, and the long process of testing began. The examination focused, essentially, on three things: the Shroud's weave, its pollen record, and its apparent bloodstains. The findings were encouraging to those who believed the Shroud to have been the burial shroud of Jesus.[12] The weave, a three-to-one herringbone twill, had parallels (although in silk) from the Greco-Roman period, and the pollen record indicated exposure in the Near East. The tests failed to produce any evidence for blood on the examined threads, but neither did they detect any residue of paint or dye. Sindonologists declared that the accusation that the Shroud's image was a fourteenth-century forgery could no longer be sustained.

The effect of these examinations, and of the half-hour presentation on television, was to stimulate rather than to satisfy public interest in the Shroud. Interest was also aroused, although in a less conspicuous way, by the debates and publications of three English sindonologists—David Willis, Maurus Green, and Ian Wilson—which were to culminate in 1978 with the publication of Wilson's *The Shroud of Turin*, an engrossing but serious book that not only has recruited thousands of readers to sindonology, but also has made remarkable contributions to the history of the Shroud.[13] To the swelling interest in the Shroud in Italy, the only appropriate response could be an exposition. When Cardinal Pellegrino retired in 1977, one of the first decisions of his successor, Archbishop Ballestrero, was to arrange for a public exposition of the Shroud, the first since 1933. The city government of Turin, which (as in many cities in Italy) was in the hands of the Communist Party, cooperated splendidly, and after so many years Turin once again had its moment in the limelight. From August 26 until October 8 of 1978 the pilgrims came, on the average of 75,000 a day, most of them reckoning that there would be no such opportunity again within their lifetime. In conjunction with the 1978 exposition, an American team of scientists was given access to the Shroud for five days, to determine as much as possible about the Shroud's age and about the nature of the image it bears. Unfortunately, permission to remove a portion of the Shroud for carbon dating, which is the most reliable method for determining the age of organic material, was not obtained, at least in part because the test requires that the material be burned (the proportion of C^{14} to C^{12} in the released gas indicates the length of time that has passed since the "death" of the organic material, which in this case would be the flax from which the linen was made). At the head of the American team were two young assistant professors from the U.S. Air Force Academy: John Jackson, a physicist, and Eric Jumper, an expert in aerodynamics, for both of whom sindonology has been a passionate avocation. The results of the 1978 tests have once again underscored the possibility that the image on the Shroud is that of Jesus.[14] At least, it is now agreed that the image could not have been painted on the linen, and that it is instead the result of an accelerated degradation or "rapid aging" of the linen fibrils. And the most recent tests, unlike those conducted in 1973, have detected evidence that the apparent bloodstains are in fact bloodstains. What is still needed, of course, is a carbon dating of the Shroud: until that is permitted there will be no scientific evidence for its age.

Responsible historians need not wait for a carbon date before reexamining the Shroud's credentials. There is no certainty, first, that the Shroud's custodians will ever release a portion of it for a carbon test. In addition, we shall see that there are some telling indications of the date of the image. Finally, Ian Wilson's proposals about the Shroud's history challenge—on the historians' own ground—Chevalier's thesis of a fourteenth-century forgery. Taken together, the arguments for the Shroud's authenticity are now serious enough that historians cannot avoid reopening a case that historians were responsible for closing eighty years ago.

ii / A Description of the Shroud and Its Image

THE Shroud is a long, rectangular piece of linen. We may assume that the cloth was once white, but now it has the color of ivory or heavy cream. On what we may call the "top" surface of the Shroud are visible the frontal and dorsal images of a man's naked body. The color of the images is a shade of brown, most often described as sepia.

More precisely, the Shroud measures 14 feet 3 inches in length, and 3 feet 7 inches in width. The entire fabric was woven in a single piece except for the left edge. Looking at the top surface, one notices a seam running down the left side of the cloth: a narrow strip, 3½ inches wide, was at some time attached to the cloth, whose original width was therefore only 3 feet 3½ inches. The image is entirely restricted to the original cloth, so it is possible that the strip was attached to the cloth after the image had been made.

The linen and the weave have been carefully studied by an expert from Belgium, Professor Gilbert Raes of the Ghent Institute of Textile Technology.[1] His microscopic examination revealed that the material of the original cloth, of the side-strip, and of the thread attaching the strip to the original cloth is all pure linen (with no admixture of wool), but that particles of cotton are caught between the threads of the original cloth. The cotton particles led Professor Raes to conclude that the loom on which the original cloth was woven had been used for weaving both linen and cotton. On the other hand, the absence of cotton particles in the side-strip suggests that the strip and the original cloth were woven on different looms. Cotton was not an uncommon fabric in the Mediterranean world in ancient times: some was grown in the Near East, some was imported from India. As for the linen itself, the weave is a three-to-one herringbone twill: in running through the warp, the weft passes under three threads and then over one, but each successive thread of the weft begins at an ascending point one thread earlier (and then, in series, at a descending point) in the pattern, producing the diagonal "herringbone" design. This particular pattern is known from antiquity as well as from the Middle Ages, although the ancient examples are silk rather than linen. It is, at any rate, a more elaborate and complicated weave than the usual over-under-over "plain" pattern, and suggests that the cloth was relatively expensive. The linen threads in the original cloth have a smaller diameter than the threads in the side-strip, again suggesting that the two pieces were woven at different times and on different looms.

Nothing like the Shroud has survived from antiquity. Hundreds of ancient textiles are extant, but none is comparable.[2] Almost without exception, the ancient textiles that exist today have all been discovered, most of them in tombs of one sort or another. A few of these cloths are in very good condition, and a few are sizable, but none can match the Shroud in both size and state of preservation. As recently as 1981, while excavating a burial from the tenth century B.C. on the Greek island of Euboea, archaeologists were happy to find a linen robe, in "astonishingly" good condition.[3] Some of the oldest linens with recognizable colored patterns come from the tomb of an Eighteenth Dynasty Egyptian king, Thutmose IV, who died in 1405 B.C. The tomb of Tutankhamen, on the other hand, yielded little cloth of value: although it contained numerous textiles (most of which were linen, and one of which shrouded the mummy), their fabric was discolored or even blackened, and some of them had all but turned to powder. Howard Carter supposed that a fungoid growth, enhanced by the tomb's heat and humidity, had led to their deterioration.[4]

That the Shroud is quite well preserved does not, however, indicate that it is of recent manufacture. It is universally agreed that the Shroud is at least six hundred years old, and during that time its deterioration seems to have been very slight. We know of other linens, prized as relics by the medieval church, that were remarkably long-lived. The so-called Holy Shroud of Besançon was at least four hundred and possibly more than fifteen hundred years old when it was destroyed in the French Revolution, for it may have been (as the faithful claimed that it was) woven in antiquity. Still another sacred linen that fell victim to the French Revolution, the Holy Shroud of Compiegne, was at least one thousand (and possibly closer to two thousand) years old at its demise, and was apparently in good repair. It had been presented as a gift to Charlemagne in 797, and was transferred to the Compiegne Abbey late in the ninth century (the Compiegne Shroud was about half the length of the Shroud of Turin, and bore no image). For all we know, had a concerted effort been made through the last two thousand years to preserve the linens of antiquity, many such linens might have survived in impressive fashion to our own time. If we leave the Shroud of Turin out of consideration, there is extant no ancient linen that has been *intentionally* preserved; those that we have, have been discovered in tombs or excavated from ancient deposits.

In scrutinizing the Shroud's credentials, experts have looked not only at its material and weave, but also at its pollen record. One of the more publicized of the tests run in 1973 was the pollen test conducted by Dr. Max Frei, who for twenty-four years had been head of the Zurich Police Scientific Laboratory. Frei's findings were not yet available when the commission published its report in 1976, and were first presented in detail in Ian Wilson's book. By removing pollen samples from the Shroud and analyzing them under a microscope, Frei attempted to identify the places in which the Shroud had stayed. Some of the reported pollens were not very interesting, since they are found in many parts of the world, and many others were typical of northern Italy and France, where the Shroud has been for the last six centuries. Other pollens that Frei identified, however, were more tantalizing. He reported finding on the Shroud pollens of a good number of halophyte desert plants from the Dead

Sea area, and of some plants restricted to the region of eastern Turkey and northeastern Syria. Finally, Frei's pollen analysis suggested that the Shroud had been exposed to the air in the region of Istanbul. We shall see in Chapter V that the conclusions reached by Dr. Frei correlate well with Ian Wilson's reconstruction of the Shroud's history. It must be noted, however, that the American team's examination in 1978 turned up very few pollens, and those that were obtained the team made no attempt to identify. Dr. Frei had hoped to confirm his earlier test with new samples in 1978, but was prevented from taking more samples when the American team objected that his procedures were too casual.[5]

The image on the Shroud is without a parallel from antiquity. Ancient shrouds displaying human images of one sort or another are sometimes claimed to have survived, but such statements are unfounded.[6] Robert Wilcox hunted down, at the Musée Guimet in Paris, the source of some of the rumors: several trunks filled with funerary textiles from a second-century burial ground in Egypt. The textiles include approximately seventy-five linen tunics, or knee-length gowns, which served as burial dresses for the corpses. Many of these tunics were stained by the decomposition of the mummies, but their stains do not at all resemble a human image.[7] On the Shroud of Besançon, mentioned above, a human image was said to have been displayed. This linen, however, was destroyed before the invention of photography, and consequently nothing can be said with certainty about its image.

What can be said about the image on the Shroud of Turin? What meets the eye is a very subtle, but unmistakable, pair of images, readily identifiable as the frontal and dorsal aspects of a man's body. If one pictures a man alive and standing erect, or an erect statue, one would imagine the cloth draped over the head, covering front and back from head to feet. Or we might picture a body (or a statue) lying on the cloth, with the feet at its left edge and the head toward its center, and we might then visualize someone bringing the unencumbered right half of the cloth over the head, and so covering the front of the body or the statue.

The figure visible on the Shroud seems tall by ancient Mediterranean standards. By the most frequently cited estimate, the Man of the Shroud was 5′11″ (181 cm.) in height, and weighed approximately 170 pounds. As usual, there is another opinion. Msgr. Giulio Ricci, archivist at the Vatican's Congregation for Bishops, after careful study concluded that the usual estimates have not sufficiently compensated for the fact that the toes of the Man of the Shroud were radically extended. According to Msgr. Ricci's estimate, the Man of the Shroud (whom the Monsignor confidently identified as Christ) was approximately 5 feet 4 inches and weighed about 155 pounds.[8]

The Man of the Shroud is bearded, has a moustache, and has long hair that is parted in the middle and falls to the shoulders. These features, needless to say, are conventional and traditional in portraits of Christ. Equally striking are what appear to be bloodstains at the wrists and ankles. As one looks at the Shroud, a stain is visible on the figure's right wrist. Because the hands are crossed over the loins, the left wrist is covered by the palm of the right hand. What seems to be a blood-streak runs up the left arm toward the elbow, just as a smaller streak on the right arm extends upward from the "blood-stained" wrist. In addition, one can see a massive stain on the figure's left side. There are also apparent rivulets of blood around the top of the head, and the dorsal image is dotted with clusters of small stains. The "wounds" of the Man of the Shroud have been analyzed often and meticulously, and one cannot deny that they correspond remarkably to the New Testament's description of Jesus' passion: the scourging, the crown of thorns, the crucifixion, the thrust of the soldier's spear into the body of Jesus—all are there to be seen on the Shroud.

The 1978 analyses, as noted in the preceding chapter, have concluded that the "bloodstains" are exactly what they seem to be.[9] Strictly speaking, the bloodstains on the image are not a part of the image. When one looks at the photographic negative of the image, these bloodstains appear as white blotches. The camera, in other words, does record a true negative image of these stains. The corollary is that on the Shroud itself the stains are not an *image* of blood, but the remains of blood. They can be explained in two ways: either the cloth was in contact with a bloodied body or, in order to simulate wounds, someone applied blood to an otherwise immaculate image.

As for the image itself, what meets the eye is intelligible, but how it was formed is a matter of vigorous debate. We shall need to review, although necessarily in a superficial way, the scientific analyses of the Shroud's image (detailed discussions, by writers competent in these matters, are available elsewhere). The battery of sophisticated and expensive tests conducted in 1978 by the Shroud of Turin Research Project (STURP) has yielded a few significant conclusions, and these have been admirably presented by L. A. Schwalbe and R. N. Rogers.[10] In addition, the results of the less extensive tests performed in 1973 have been available for some time.[11] Taken together, the two series of tests have not been as productive and conclusive as many interested parties had hoped. But although much remains unclear, considerably more is known now than was known when the Shroud was shown on television in 1973.

Most important, perhaps, is the consensus that the image was not painted on the cloth. This is now conceded by virtually every observer, even those who believe that the image is somehow the result of human artifice. Painters outline a figure before painting it, but there is no tell-tale outline on the Shroud. Nor is there a hint of the directionality that brush-marks would produce. Finally, there is no clear evidence of any pigment on the Shroud, although here there is some disagreement. The STURP team, using microscopic, chemical laser microprobes, concluded that the Shroud shows no trace of "any of the expected dyes, stains, pigments, or painting media."[12] A sometime member of the team, however, concluded otherwise. Walter C. McCrone, who is one of America's most respected forensic microanalysts, reported finding submicrometer-sized particles of iron oxide throughout the image area, but not on the clear area of the Shroud.[13] This ferric oxide, McCrone concluded, was residue of a rouge, similar to today's Venetian Red, that was used by ancient and medieval painters. Two other investigators, John Heller and A. D. Adler, conceded the presence of iron on the Shroud, but flatly disagreed with McCrone's analysis. According to Heller and Adler, a microspectrophotometer showed that most of the iron was blood porphyrin. A small percentage of the iron occurred in iron oxide, they reported, but the iron oxide was not a pigment: it occurred throughout the Shroud on the periphery of water stains, and must have resulted from the 1532 fire at Chambéry.[14] However the iron oxide particles are to be explained, it is agreed that they did not "produce" the image. In his recently published *Inquest on the Shroud of Turin,* Joe Nickell emphasizes the iron oxide, and upon it builds his case that the Shroud was forged in the fourteenth century by an artist who used a printing procedure. Nickell's observations deserve to be taken seriously, even though they rest on rather limited experiments. (Nickell, who once was a resident magician at the Houdini Magical Hall of Fame, has assembled his own "panel of scientific and technical experts" to challenge the conclusions of the STURP team.) It is therefore noteworthy that even Nickell excludes the possibility that the image was painted, and concedes that "ferric oxide contributes less than about 10 percent to the overall image intensity."[15]

If the image on the Shroud does not (except possibly to a very small degree) consist of a pigment, stain, or dye, of what does it consist? Another welcome development within the last five years has been a general agreement about the nature of the image. Both Nickell's associates and the STURP scientists who have studied it have concluded that the light brown or sepia color of the image fibers is the result of the accelerated degradation of those fibers.[16] How the degradation came about remains a puzzle, but at least the immediate "cause" of the image has been explained. Linen, like paper or other tissues made from plants, consists of cellulose, and cellulose is subject to various chemical changes that discolor it, turning the white color to some shade between yellow and brown. Thus, a typical fiber of the Shroud in the image area appears sepia, even though no sepia dye or pigment was applied to the cloth. On such a typical fiber, only the topmost fibrils have suffered discoloration, and one may therefore safely conclude that whatever it was that produced the image must have affected only the surface fibrils; the process did not penetrate to the reverse side of the cloth.

The main question still unanswered is, what caused the degradation of the surface fibrils in the image area? A traditional belief that has been rephrased in scientific terminology associates the image with Jesus' resurrection: the infusion of life into Jesus' dead body resulted in "a very short burst of high-energy radiation."[17] The STURP scientists are not inclined to accept this particiular explanation, since their experiments along those lines either destroyed the test fabric or, at best, resulted in images that penetrated to the reverse side of the cloths.[18] But since scientists cannot effect a resurrection, it is not necessarily significant that they are unable to duplicate one of its supposed side-effects.

A somewhat broader theory is that the Shroud's image is the result of a scorch, either by direct contact or by radiation across a distance of one or two centimeters. The arguments supporting some kind of "scorch" hypothesis are fairly impressive. To the naked eye, in both color and character the image resembles the outer edge of those portions of the cloth that definitely *were* scorched by a fire in 1532. Second, laboratory analyses have shown that the known scorches share with the image certain optical properties, and "ultraviolet and visible light reflectance tests showed that the image and the fire scorches reflected light in a similar way."[19] Finally, an experiment done in 1961 by Mr. Geoffrey Ashe, in Maidstone, England, showed that a scorch can produce an image that not only reproduces details as small as an eighth of an inch, but that also, when photographed, yields a positive image on the photographic negative.[20]

The "scorch" theory has several variations (even the "burst of radiation" at the moment of resurrection would be a scorch). One version, proposed and examined from time to time, is that a stone or metal statue was heated to a moderate temperature, and that the Shroud was then pressed upon it or tented over it. Experiments by Eric Jumper and John Jackson, however, "have shown that three-dimensional hot-statue hypotheses are rather unlikely."[21]

Just as the word "photographic" describes a process in which light creates an image, the word "thermographic" would be appropriate when an image is created by heat. Any hypothesis of a scorch—whether resulting from a burst of energy or from some human procedure—entails what we might call a kind of thermography. Of the various scorches that might have produced the Shroud's image, radiation seems more likely than direct contact, and a relatively slow process more likely than a sudden burst. As Schwalbe and Rogers have summarized the research on scorches, "at this time, the most likely scorch hypothesis is that the Shroud image is a light 'air' scorch produced at temperatures lower than those sufficient to carbonize the material."[22]

Scorching is not the only method of degrading linen fibers. Their color can also be turned to yellow or brown by the application of sulfuric or some other acid. Such a procedure, however, almost invariably affects far more than the surface fibrils. In addition, the application of an acid could not produce the "three-dimensional" image apparent on the Shroud, and that a radiation scorch can produce. The image on the Shroud, that is, presents the bodily features in depth, or in a "global" fashion: the recessed eye-sockets, for example, contrast sharply with the brows and with the ridge of the nose.

The Shroud's image has also been explained as a result of a "sensitizing" of the cloth by the application of foreign substances. The areas thus sensitized would age more rapidly than the rest of the cloth, and the yellow or brown cellulose eventually would appear as an "image" against those parts of the cloth that have not been sensitized. S. F. Pellicori explored this "latent image theory" and published his results in *Archaeology*, the popular periodical of the Archaeological Institute of America.[23] His supposition was that the Shroud may have been sensitized by contact with a body—whether the body of Jesus or of someone else—and that over the decades and centuries the latent image may have "developed." In his experiment, Pellicori applied a mixture of myrrh, olive oil, and skin secretions to a linen cloth. Then, instead of waiting the required decades or centuries for the image to appear, Pellicori substituted for the natural aging of the linen a "rapid aging process": he baked the cloth for three and a half hours, at a temperature of 300° F (150° C), and found that an image did appear on the linen. Finally, he washed off the mixture of myrrh, olive oil, and skin secretions. The image remained indelibly on the fibers that the mixture had sensitized.

Although Pellicori proposed that his theory demonstrated how the Shroud's image might have arisen "naturally" over the centuries,[24] the result neither of human art nor of a miracle, the "latent image theory" obviously has other uses. One could argue that however "natural" the mechanism might be, the fact that it occurred in this single instance is something of a miracle, after all. One could also argue that the mechanism described by Pellicori fits very well with an artificial origin of the image. Someone in ancient or medieval times could have done exactly what Pellicori did: bake a sensitized cloth until the "development" of the desired image. Pellicori himself observed that the linen could be sensitized by a wide variety of agents, his particular choice (myrrh, olive oil, and skin secretions) having depended on his assumptions about Christ's burial. But if the Shroud's image is intentional and man-made, any one of a number of substances (soapwort, for example), might have been used by an imprinter to produce the same results as Pellicori's mixture.

Pellicori's proposal has made an important contribution to sindonology. In its favor is the fact, concisely stated by Schwalbe and Rogers, "that Pellicori's latent image process has provided the closest approximation to the color and chemical properties of the image."[25] Against the theory is the lack of three-dimensionality in the image. Schwalbe and Rogers do not, however, on that account rule out the theory, suggesting that "although the spatial gradation of image density . . . does not result in an obvious manner from simple contact models, there may be some possibilities."[26] The latent image theory is therefore an incomplete explanation. It will be compelling only if some additional physical mechanism is found to account for the density shadings on the image.

It must also be emphasized that as it stands, Pellicori's theory does not by itself exclude either an artificial or a "natural" origin of the Shroud's image. One might believe that a burial shroud was sensitized by contact with (or proximity to) Jesus' body, and that the image of Jesus "developed" on its own over the decades and centuries, to the utter amazement of the Shroud's custodians. We might, on the other hand, imagine that someone intentionally sensitized the cloth by bringing it into contact with (or proximity to) a suitably prepared human body, and then brought out the latent image by baking the cloth.

Yet another kind of experiment has been publicized by Joe Nickell. Some years ago Nickell decided that the Shroud's image had been made in roughly the same manner that brass rubbings are made from grave slabs. After several unsuccessful attempts, Nickell stretched a canvas around a small frame, coated his face with brownish rouge, and "pulled a print" from his own face. The print, like all prints, was in essence a negative. "A photographer's negative produced a positive image remarkable for its clarity. Even the texture of the moustache is revealed."[27] The illustrations that accompanied Nickell's account of all this in *The Humanist* do indeed show a photographic negative that is much clearer and much more a "positive" than the original image, and Nickell clearly demonstrated that the "negativity" of the Shroud's image may have a fairly simple explanation. The problem with Nickell's first experiment was the distortion of the facial features and the fact that on his canvas the image consisted of an applied substance—the brown rouge—whereas on the Shroud's image, there is at most a bare trace of an applied substance. In his subsequent publications, therefore, Nickell has proposed a somewhat different procedure: the four-teenth-century artist first sculpted a low bas-relief of a man's body, then powdered it with rouge, and finally printed the cloth. The ferric oxide of the rouge, when moistened, would degrade and yellow the cellulose fibrils, and the image would remain after the rouge had been washed from the cloth.[28] Nickell's suggestions about the origins of the Shroud's image have not persuaded Schwalbe and Rogers, however; they object that because there "seems to be no historical evidence to suggest that any such technique was used before the 19th century," Nickell's method "may at best represent a unique and subsequently forgotten innovation."[29]

All the recent scientific analyses point to some modification of the cellulose structure, whether by a scorch or by sensitization and "aging," as the process that produced the image. It must be conceded, however, that there is not yet a satisfactory explanation of how the Shroud's image was made, much less a successful duplication of that image. Experimentation is continuing and should be encouraged. A carbon test can furnish us with a date for the Shroud, and therefore a presumption about the date of its image. But how the image was created and when it was created are two completely unrelated questions. It is theoretically possible that the image was created by human artifice almost two thousand years ago, or that it originated in a miraculous burst of light in 1350.

Experiments do not, nor can they in the future, show that the Shroud's image originated with a miracle. By definition, nothing that science can explain is inexplicable, and the conclusions that sindonologists can expect from science must invariably be limited either to "natural" or to artificial processes. Perhaps at this point—most (though not quite all) of the scientific tests having already been completed—one must look to history rather than to science for further answers. History cannot prove that the Shroud's image is or is not miraculous, but examining the Shroud's history can perhaps help one to decide which alternative is the more likely. Some of the matters discussed in this chapter—the Shroud's material, its weave, its pollen record— have had an important bearing on the Shroud's history. And another scientific test—a Carbon 14 dating of the cloth—may in the future make a decisive contribution to our knowledge of the Shroud's history. But in addition to asking where the Shroud has been, and how old it is, we must also ask how people have regarded it. A knowledgeable estimate of the Shroud and its image will be informed by the statements and beliefs of those who may have known more about it than is known today.

iii / The Identity of the Man of the Shroud

THE Shroud has traditionally been advertised as the burial shroud of Jesus Christ, and the frontal and dorsal images upon it have traditionally been claimed as the *vera imago*, the "true image" of Jesus, directly imprinted by his body. Since the first public display of the Shroud in the small French town of Lirey, during the 1350s, the Shroud's admirers have not wavered in their convictions about its nature and origin. It might therefore seem that those who deny that the Shroud's image is the true image of Jesus are obliged to bring forward their evidence: the burden of proof should logically fall on the sceptics, since they have seen fit to contest the received opinion. The defendant, after all, is innocent unless proven guilty.

In this instance, however, the roles of plaintiff and defendant are not what they seem to be. The "received opinion" that is important, at least as far as we are concerned, is that which prevails not among the membership of the Holy Shroud Guild, but among professional historians. And since historians have traditionally presumed that the claim for the Shroud is a fiction, the burden of proof falls on those who believe that the Shroud does indeed bear the true image of Jesus.

Before seeing what sort of case the believers can present, we must nonetheless acknowledge that the sceptics' case would today be more difficult to make than it was when Chevalier and Thurston were writing. Those scholars rested their case primarily on a memorandum written in 1389 by Pierre d'Arcis, bishop of Troyes, to Pope Clement VII in Avignon. Bishop d'Arcis was distressed that "a certain cloth cunningly painted" was once again exhibited in his diocese and was popularly regarded as "the actual shroud in which our Savior Jesus Christ was enfolded in the tomb, and upon which the whole likeness of the Saviour has remained thus impressed together with the wounds that he bore."[1] The Shroud had first been displayed some thirty years earlier, and had immediately attracted attention not only in all of France, but also "so to speak, throughout the world." D'Arcis went on to recount how the then bishop of Troyes, Bishop Henri, was told by the theologians and other wise men that the claim for the Shroud could not be true,

> since the holy Gospel made no mention of any such imprint, while, if it had been true, it was quite unlikely that the holy Evangelists would have omitted to record it, or that the fact should have remained hidden until the present time. Eventually, after diligent inquiry and examination, he discovered the fraud and how the said cloth had been cunningly painted, the truth being attested by the artist who had painted it, to wit, that it was a work of human skill and not miraculously wrought or bestowed.

It is this memorandum of Bishop d'Arcis that Chevalier called to the world's attention in 1900 and on which the sceptics' case formally rests.

From the very beginning, Bishop d'Arcis's testimony raised certain questions. If someone in the 1350s had publicly confessed to having manufactured the Shroud's image, why did pilgrims flock to see the Shroud when it was again exhibited in 1389? And is it likely that such a monstrous hoax—the counterfeiting of Christ's burial shroud—could have been perpetrated in the 1350s, when Lirey and all Europe were recovering from the Black Death, and when religious fears and fervor ran high? Furthermore, one would not expect Geoffrey de Charny, who in the early 1350s owned the Shroud and who built the Lirey church, of complicity in a forgery. Geoffrey was not only one of the kingdom's most trusted and gallant knights, but also a seemingly devout author of religious poetry.[2] Finally, it appears that neither Pope Clement VII nor Bishop d'Arcis's successor in the diocese of Troyes was persuaded that the Shroud was a fraud.

Arguments such as these are troublesome, but are not sufficient to undermine Bishop d'Arcis's statement that Bishop Henri had obtained a confession from the man who painted the Shroud's image. Recently, several other difficulties have emerged. First, the wounds that appear on the image seem more authentic than they did eighty years ago. The American scientists' conclusion "that the Shroud 'blood' areas are blood"[3] does not by itself mean very much, since at any time in the Shroud's early history someone might have added bloodstains to the original image. More important is the location of the wounds: the "blood-flow" on the arms of the Man of the Shroud originates at the wrists, and not at the palms of the hands. In fourteenth-century France, as elsewhere in medieval Europe, artists depicted the crucified Christ suspended from nails driven through the palms of the hands. The wrist-wounds of the Man of the Shroud intrigued Pierre Barbet, and in his *A Doctor at Calvary* Barbet argued that the Shroud's testimony was more credible than the artistic convention. Barbet buttressed his opinion with an account of experiments that he had done with cadavers: a body cannot be suspended from nails driven through the palms, for the weight of the body tears the palms immediately, whereas a body can be suspended indefinitely from nails driven through the wrists.[4] Barbet's gruesome observations were strengthened in 1968, when for the first time archaeologists happened upon the skeleton of a victim of crucifixion. In that year Israeli archaeologists excavated a first-century cemetery at Giv'at ha-Mivtar, near Jerusalem.[5] Among the skeletons was that of a man whose name, according to an accompanying inscription, was Jehohanan, and Jehohanan had clearly been crucified.[6] A heavy, five-inch nail transfixed one or both of Jehohanan's heel-bones, and his legs had been broken. The radius bones of Jehohanan's arms were damaged at the wrist end, indicating to Dr. Nicu Haas, the specialist in physical anthropology who studied and published all of the Giv'at ha-Mivtar skeletal remains, that Jehohanan had been suspended on his cross from nails driven through the forearm just above the wrist. If the Shroud is a fourteenth-century forgery, it is surprising that the forger knew enough about the details of crucifixion (a method of execution that in Bishop Henri's time had been forbidden for a thousand years) to contradict the unanimous opinion of medieval Christians that nails had been driven through the middle of Jesus' palms.

The most serious difficulty with Bishop d'Arcis's characterization of the Shroud as a forgery is his remark that Bishop Henri found out who had painted the image, the affair being divulged "by the artist who had painted it." Today it is quite certain that the image was not painted. Therefore, although it is possible that somebody "confessed" to Bishop Henri that he had painted the image, we can no longer put much stock in such a confession. One could, of course, argue that Bishop d'Arcis was perhaps careless in using the word "painted" (*depinxit*) and that perhaps he meant to use a broader verb, such as "created" or "produced." Here, too, there are objections. If an ingenious Frenchman in the fourteenth century invented a process for producing something as senational as the Shroud, which d'Arcis says was causing a stir throughout not only France but the whole world, it is hard to understand why the forger did not use the process again. The wealth that the little church in Lirey was accumulating ought to have inspired the forger, or someone privy to his trade secrets, to produce shrouds of apostles, saints, and martyrs. But there is no evidence that anyone, in France or anywhere else, was able to duplicate the Shroud being exhibited in Lirey. One must then resort to the argument that arts can be lost: rare techniques, known to only a few persons, may not survive those practitioners. Although this is theoretically true, and would have some validity if one were dealing with an art or technique from the ancient, Classical world (so much, after all, was lost in the Dark Age), it would be difficult to find any example of an art that became extinct just when its product was exciting all the world.

In short, sceptics can no longer rest their case on Bishop d'Arcis's statement that in the 1350s Bishop Henri discovered who had painted the image on the Shroud. Bishop Henri found it incredible that the burial shroud of Jesus was in the little church in Lirey; today it is even more incredible that one of Bishop Henri's contemporaries painted the Shroud's image.

It is fortunate for the sceptics, then, that the burden of proof is no longer on their shoulders. The learned consensus remains that the Shroud is a hoax, even though the basis for that consensus has been eroded. That the Shroud carries the true image of Jesus is simply an assertion, although repeated for centuries, that historians need not accept unless it rests on a persuasive argument. Let us see whether such an argument can be made.

The conventional argument that the image on the Shroud is the true image of Jesus assumes that we all agree, as perhaps we may, that the image came from a dead man's body. Most reasonable investigators have firmly ruled out the possibility that the image was painted, and they are also persuaded that it could not have been effected by means of a scorch from a hot statue. In addition, experts in anatomy and forensic medicine have concluded that the image on the Shroud could only have come from a human body, and in fact from the body of a man who had died (rigor mortis is evident) the violent death indicated by the visible wounds. These conclusions, as we have seen, were first reported by Delage in his 1902 address to the French Academy, and they have often been confirmed: in greatest detail by physician Pierre Barbet, and most recently by Robert Bucklin, deputy medical examiner of Los Angeles County in California.[7]

In addition to this reasonable assumption, the argument that the image came from Jesus' body assumes—and here we might disagree—that the image was not produced by human skill, but is either miraculous (if it is Jesus' image) or "natural" (if it is someone else's image). If this second assumption is conceded, the argument quickly and inexorably narrows to the desired conclusion. Of the millions who died in antiquity, a tiny minority died of crucifixion. Of the thousands of men who were crucified, only a few hundred would have been wrapped in a linen sheet, as the Gospels say that Jesus was. Of these few hundred buried in a shroud, only a fraction would have been scourged before crucifixion, as was Jesus and as was the Man of the Shroud. And of those who suffered those tortures, how many would have been wounded across the scalp, as though by a crown of thorns? How many bodies so abused were pierced in the side by a spear? And of all the bodies that meet these requirements, how many—here the odds rise to the maximum—would have been separated from their shrouds before decomposition began?

In a recent book, *Verdict on the Shroud*, Gary Habermas thus fixes the statistical probability that a body other than Jesus' has left its imprint on the Shroud.[8] Others have made the attempt before, and Habermas notes their conclusions: reckonings of the chance that a body, if it leaves an imprint at all, will leave *this* imprint, range from 1 in 225,000,000,000, at the lower end of the scale, to 1 in 10^{26} at the higher. Habermas's own estimate is a much more conservative 1 in 82,944,000.

These odds, however, are far too high, and the argument is misleading. For, as suggested above, the assumption that the Shroud's image was not wrought by men is invalid. The failure to find a significant residue of paint, dye or ink on the Shroud does not necessarily mean that someone did not produce the image, using an imprinting or thermographic technique that has since been lost. Let us estimate the likelihood (obviously, we cannot indulge in statistics here) that someone, at some time, using a corpse that had been appropriately bloodied and disfigured, set out to produce an image that would correspond precisely to the Gospels' account of Jesus' passion.

We have already seen that a forgery in the fourteenth century is unlikely: a European of that time would have placed nail-wounds in the hands of the corpse, and the technique that produced the Shroud would, in the fourteenth century, have been much too valuable to lapse into oblivion. These objections do not, however, apply to an earlier period in Western history: late antiquity, especially the third and fourth centuries. Criminals were still executed by crucifixion in the early fourth century, and undoubtedly for some decades thereafter the details of this type of execution were remembered. And an exotic technique for imprinting a human image on cloth, we shall see, was apparently known in antiquity but had been lost by the sixth century. One might thus propose that the Shroud's image was produced in the third or fourth century, or early in the fifth. Of the many Christian writers of late antiquity, not one mentions a cloth bearing an image of Jesus' crucified body. We may therefore be certain that if the Shroud's image *was* produced in late antiquity, it failed to attract much attention. The procedure that produced the image, however clever it may have been, might well have lapsed in the face of such indifference. If the Shroud's image was created, through some now-lost process of imprinting or thermography, as an imitation of Christ's crucified body, it is far more likely to have been created in late antiquity than in the late Middle Ages.

In the last analysis, however, we must concede that even an ancient forgery is unlikely. A fourth-century craftsman who intended to produce an image of Jesus would probably not have pictured Jesus' face as the face that is familiar to us in Christian art, and that we see in the Shroud. In late antiquity Jesus was occasionally represented as a bearded man with shoulder-length hair, parted in the middle, but he was more often pictured as a youthful, beardless, round-faced man, in the tradition of an Apollo or a young Hermes. This is hardly a decisive argument against the manufacture of the Shroud's image in late antiquity, but it nonetheless does carry some weight. In assigning the Shroud's image to late antiquity, a far greater difficulty than its form is its content: on the Shroud we see a crucified body, naked and bloody, and Christians in late antiquity never depicted Jesus naked or dead. In fact, early Christian art did not even portray Jesus on the cross.[9] The earliest known representation of the crucifixion of Jesus is a panel on the wooden door of Santa Sabina in Rome, carved ca. 432, and the subject remained a great rarity until the eighth century. One of the early examples appears in the Rabbula Codex, an illuminated Syriac manuscript dating ca. 586, and there Jesus is portrayed, incongruously, fully clothed while hanging on the cross.[10] In the third and fourth centuries Christians restricted themselves to depicting Jesus as a teacher, a miracle-worker, a shepherd, or as Christ in Triumph. The passion was not a subject that Christians had any desire to visualize. That some Christian in late antiquity should have decided to create, on a fourteen-foot sheet of linen, an imitation of the frontal and dorsal images of the naked body of the crucified Jesus is unimaginable.

Could, then, the image have been created in late antiquity by a pagan, hostile to Christianity and not above desecrating Jesus' passion by making a grotesque facsimile of his burial shroud? This is a possibility (a graffito has survived that satirizes the crucifixion), although one remote enough that we need not long consider it. What purpose such an anti-Christian might have had is not easy to imagine. A reasonably perceptive pagan should have had the sense to foresee that the image would serve only to verify, for Christians, the entire tradition of Jesus' passion, burial, and resurrection.

In short, it is quite improbable that anyone, whether in the Middle Ages or in antiquity, whether a Christian or an opponent of Christianity, created the Shroud's image in order to simulate the image of Jesus' crucified body. Nor is there any statistical probability at all that the Shroud bears a nonintentional, or "natural," image of a body other than Jesus' body. We must therefore conclude that, if the Shroud is indeed ancient, as it seems to be, it is very likely that the image on the Shroud is that of Jesus' body. Should a carbon test indicate that the Shroud itself dates from around the time of Jesus, the probability will be overwhelming that what we have on the Shroud is the *vera imago* of Jesus.

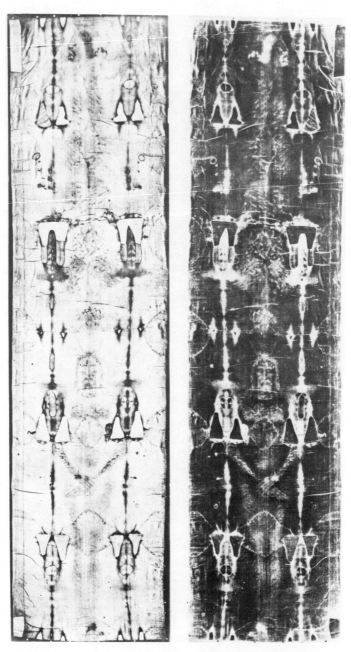

Plate 1. The Shroud of Turin: positive and negative images of the entire Shroud. *Left:* the Shroud as it appears to the naked eye; *right:* the Shroud as seen in a photographic negative. (Holy Shroud Guild)

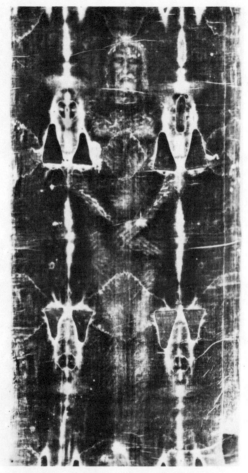

Plate 2. Frontal aspect of the Man of the Shroud, negative image. (Holy Shroud Guild)

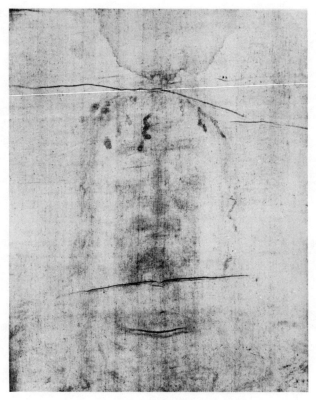

Plate 3. Positive image of the face of the Man of the Shroud. (Holy Shroud Guild)

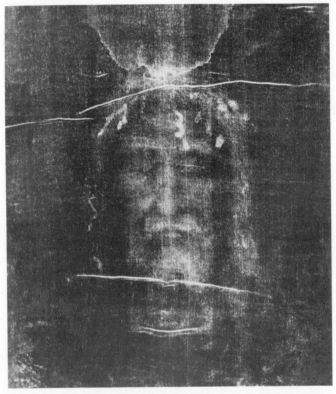

Plate 4. Negative image of the face of the Man of the Shroud. (Holy Shroud Guild)

Plate 5. The "Good Shepherd." Painting from the Tomb of the Aurelii, in Rome. Ca. 250. (Pont. Comm. di Arch. Sacra)

Plate 6. Christ Healing the Woman with an Issue of Blood. Painting from the Catacomb of Saints Peter and Marcellinus, in Rome. Ca. 275. (Pont. Comm. di Arch. Sacra)

Plate 7. Bust of Christ. Painting from the Catacomb of Commodilla, in Rome. Ca. 350. (Pont. Comm. di Arch. Sacra)

Plate 8. Christ Between Peter and Paul. Painting in the Catacomb of Saints Peter and Marcellinus, in Rome. Ca. 375. (Pont. Comm. di Arch. Sacra)

Plate 9. Christ Enthroned. Apse mosaic, San Vitale, Ravenna. Ca. 545. (Art Resource)

Plate 10. Painting of the Mandylion, at Gradac, Serbia. 13th century. (Grabar, *La Sainte Face de Laon*)

Plate 11. Painting of the Mandylion, at Spas Nereditsa (near Novgorod), Russia. 1199. (Grabar, *La Sainte Face de Laon*)

iv / The Mandylion

W HEN Bishop Henri asked the theologians and wise men of his day whether they thought that the Shroud was authentic, they replied that they did not. Their skepticism was based not on the Shroud's appearance, but on its lack of any *history*. How, they asked, could something so astounding, and of such supreme importance, have gone unnoticed and unmentioned for more than thirteen centuries, only to turn up suddenly in an undistinguished French hamlet? No matter how authentic the Shroud might have looked, scholars rejected it because it had no past.

This gap, fatal to the Shroud's credibility, has recently been filled. Ian Wilson, in the course of several ingenious chapters in his *Shroud of Turin*, supplies a history of the Shroud from Jesus' burial to the present.[1] Not all of Wilson's reconstruction is persuasive, but the main framework of the Shroud's history now seems to be in place, and this is an accomplishment of extraordinary importance. What Wilson has contributed to sindonology is no less—and probably more—significant than the recent scientific findings.

In essence, Wilson has made a very strong case that throughout the Middle Ages the Shroud was revered by Christians of the Byzantine East as the Mandylion, an unspeakably sacred cloth. From 944 until it disappeared soon after Crusaders sacked the city in 1204, the Mandylion was kept in one of the emperor's chapels in Constantinople, and it had earlier been the pride and treasure of Edessa, a city near the northeastern border of Syria. According to Christian tradition, the cloth had been brought to

Edessa by a royal official, Ananias, shortly before Jesus' passion. By identifying it with the Mandylion, Wilson thus gives the Shroud a history that stretches back at least to the early Middle Ages, and possibly to the Apostolic Age.

Anyone who attempts to reconstruct the Shroud's history must work backward from the present to its origin. The most recent segment of the Shroud's history—from its exposition at Lirey in the 1350s to the present—is the least controversial. The Shroud remained the property of the de Charny family through three generations, and was frequently moved about, to prevent its falling into the hands of Englishmen or brigands. Shortly before she died in 1460, Margaret de Charny, granddaughter of the knight killed at Poitiers, gave the Shroud to Duke Louis of Savoy, and from that time until 1983 it was the property of the House of Savoy. In 1578 Duke Emmanuel Philibert moved his palace to Turin, and the Shroud went with him. It was deposited in the House of Savoy's chapel at San Giovanni Battista in 1694. It has been in Turin ever since (except for emergencies, such as World War II), and has there long survived the House of Savoy, which became the royal house of Italy in 1861 and remained so until 1946, when King Umberto II went into exile.

But while the Shroud's whereabouts since the 1350s are in no doubt, the same cannot be said about its history before Geoffrey de Charny built his little church in Lirey. Before publication of Wilson's book, there was only vague speculation about where the Shroud might have been before the fourteenth century. Although there is still no certainty, thanks to Wilson's careful but imaginative research we now have a plausible and even persuasive explanation of the fact that before the 1350s Christendom did not seem to know of a burial shroud showing the true image of Jesus' body: earlier Christians had known the Shroud as the Mandylion.

The identification of the Shroud with the Mandylion of Byzantium seems so reasonable, now that Wilson has argued in its behalf, that one wonders why it had not occurred to others. But we must recall that until a few years ago most historians supposed that the Shroud had been painted in the fourteenth century. Wilson, on the other hand, convinced that

the Shroud was not a fourteenth-century forgery, was compelled
to hunt for traces of its earlier existence. His search led him
very quickly to the Mandylion.

Initially, the identification seems preposterous. The word
mandylion means, literally, "little towel" or "little handkerchief."
Byzantine artists' paintings of the Mandylion indicated that it
was a cloth about the size of a large bath towel, and both the
paintings and the literary accounts portray it as bearing an
imprint not of Jesus' crucified body, but of the living Jesus' face.
Although there were varying accounts of how the image was
imprinted on the Mandylion, the most widely circulated story
was as follows:[2] when Jesus was still on this earth, King Abgar
of Edessa heard of his miracles and teaching, and sent one of
his subjects, Ananias, both to invite the Lord to Edessa and to
bring back a portrait of him. Jesus replied with a letter to Abgar,
explaining that he could not come to Edessa since his mission
was to remain among the Jews. When Ananias tried, with little
success, to sketch Jesus' portrait (the glory of Jesus' countenance
went beyond the artist's powers), Jesus washed his face and
pressed a cloth to it, miraculously imprinting an image of his
face on the cloth. The face of Christ on the Mandylion is well
known in Christian art: although the relic itself was lost in the
early thirteenth century, artists had by that time painted copies
of it in many churches in the Orthodox East, from Athens to
Novgorod.

Several sindonologists, and especially Paul Vignon, had long
ago called attention to some striking similarities between the
face on the Shroud and the face of Jesus as depicted in the
Byzantine world and in certain traditions in western Europe
(especially in Italy) from the seventh century to the twelfth.
Everyone can see that the Man of the Shroud, like the Christ
in most Christian art, is bearded and has long hair, parted down
the middle of the head and falling to the shoulders. Such
similarities mean nothing, since even if the Shroud were a
fourteenth-century forgery it would presumably portray Christ
in that way. More interesting were the subtler similarities, ranging
from the two wisps of hair at the top of the forehead, to the
fork of the beard. Most important, however, were those char-

acteristics of the Christ face in Byzantine and early medieval art that were paralleled by a *fortuitous* mark on the Shroud: a "wrinkle-line" in the cloth, for example, or an imperfection in the weave, or an apparent blemish. Here, clearly, one could not argue that the image on the Shroud was copied from earlier Christian art, and the alternative was that the face on the Shroud had been the source of certain medieval and Byzantine traditions of Christ-portraits. In a 1939 book Vignon itemized what he thought were the salient peculiarities, and others followed his lead. An American priest, Father Edward Wuenschel, and an English Benedictine, Fr. Maurus Green, extended the list. On Wilson's tabulation, no less than fifteen "peculiarities" can be explained only by derivation from the Shroud.[3]

In this argument the Mandylion of Byzantium was important, but not central. Both Vignon and Wuenschel supposed that the Mandylion was just one of several famous Byzantine or medieval European Christ-portraits inspired by the Shroud. They did not, of course, question the common assumption that the Mandylion was a portrait painted by an artist, that it was painted on a rather small cloth, and that it was limited to Jesus' face. For Vignon and Wuenschel the Mandylion, like some of the portraits of Jesus in the catacombs, testified to the existence of the Shroud from late antiquity through the twelfth century. But where the Shroud may have been, during that time, remained a riddle.

It was left to Ian Wilson to make the brilliant deduction that Mandylion and Shroud were one and the same. Like his predecessors, Wilson recognized that the face on the Shroud resembled, in remarkable ways, the face of Jesus in the Mandylion tradition. What intrigued him, however, was the persistent claim of Orthodox Christians that the Mandylion was an *acheiropoietos* icon, an image "not made by hands." That, of course, is how millions of Catholics have, for the last six hundred years, regarded the Shroud. Discussing the matter with Maurus Green, Wilson suggested that the Mandylion may not have been a painted portrait after all. The adjective *acheiropoietos* implied that the Mandylion had not looked like a portrait, and the image most certainly had been on a linen cloth. In addition, the image was said to have looked as though it had been formed by a moist secretion, and it was also said to have been dim and difficult to perceive. Was it not possible, Wilson speculated, that the Mandylion was the Shroud?

Exploring in more detail the traditions about the Mandylion, Wilson soon found evidence that supported his hunch. First, there had apparently been bloodstains on the Mandylion. The generally accepted story of the imprint's origin was that Jesus had pressed the cloth to his face after an ordinary day during his ministry. But the alternative story, Wilson observed, was that Jesus imprinted his image on the cloth when, in the Garden of Gethsemane, "his sweat was as it were great drops of blood, falling down to the ground" (Luke 22:44). This second story of the Mandylion's origins convinced Wilson that on the Mandylion face, as on the Shroud face, were what worshippers thought to be drops of blood.

Wilson learned that not only the image on the Mandylion, but the cloth itself strikingly paralleled the Shroud. The color of the Mandylion, as of the Shroud, was off-white or ivory. And the Mandylion had had an unusual shape for a portrait: the face of Jesus was centered in a horizontal rectangle—about the width of the Shroud—despite the preference of artists of all ages and societies to center a face in an upright rectangle (see Plate 10). Most important was Wilson's discovery that the Mandylion had been mounted and framed.[4] This was suggested, first of all, by the twelfth-century paintings of the Mandylion, which picture not a loosely suspended cloth, but one stretched and taut. The crucial details Wilson found in a sermon on the Mandylion, written soon after the icon was brought from Edessa to Constantinople in 944.[5] The tenth-century author of this "Festival Sermon" told how Jesus had sent the sacred cloth, bearing his divine imprint, to King Abgar of Edessa, who had invited the Savior to leave Judaea and come to Edessa. Immediately after receiving the sacred cloth, the tenth-century author continued, King Abgar arranged for it to be venerated, "fastening it to a board and embellishing it with the gold which is now to be seen." The gold-work to which the author referred, Wilson reasoned, was undoubtedly the trellis-like golden encasement that appears time and again in paintings of the

Mandylion. This encasement, which framed the nimbus of the divine face, seems to have been something like a slip-cover, or jacket, embroidered with a trellis- or net-pattern in gold thread (see Plates 10 and 11). Some of the paintings, Wilson observed, suggest that the embroidered jacket had a fringe, and that this fringe was tacked to the board against which the Mandylion seems to have been mounted. If Shroud and Mandylion were the same thing, then the Shroud may have been folded and tightly packed against the board, the jacket with its circular cut-out holding the cloth in place and permitting the worshipper to see the face of the Shroud's image.

That the Mandylion was merely the exposed section of a much larger cloth was, Wilson found, corroborated by an unusual noun in a sixth-century text entitled *The Acts of Thaddaeus*. This text, which contains the earliest version we have of what became the traditional story of the origin of the sacred image, reports that Jesus

> asked to wash himself, and a *tetradiplon* was given to him; and when he had washed himself he wiped his face with it. And his image having been imprinted upon the linen . . .[6]

The word *tetradiplon* is a very unusual term, and Wilson's inquiries concluded that the word appeared nowhere else in classical or Byzantine Greek literature. But although strange, it is a perfectly understandable word, since it is a compound of two very ordinary Greek words: *tetra,* meaning "four," and *diplon,* "doubled." The cloth which the author of *The Acts of Thaddaeus* had in mind was apparently doubled, or folded, four times. Wilson conjectured that the front panel of the Mandylion was a surface one-eighth the length of the whole: the linen had been arranged in eight folds, of which one was partially exposed to the viewer, and the other seven were entirely encased between the slip-cover and the board. Anyone permitted to handle the icon might have been able to touch the folds, and so to count them, but would probably have supposed that they were nothing but blank linen.

* * *

When Wilson first presented his hypothesis there was no

physical evidence to support it. Since then, it has been reported that with high magnification, photographs do show signs of eight folds where Wilson's theory requires them to be.[7] Even without that photographic evidence, however, there is reason to think that Wilson's identification of the Shroud with the Mandylion is correct (if a carbon test should prove the Shroud to be ancient, the identification would be established beyond any reasonable doubt). In fact, several literary texts not cited by Wilson squarely support his thesis.

We can be certain, first of all, that the Mandylion together with its encasement was a fairly bulky object. This is suggested in a text edited by Ernst von Dobschuetz that he labeled "The Liturgical Tractate,"[8] composed ca. 960. This "Liturgical Tractate" described for the benefit of the Constantinopolitan hierarchy the rituals by which the sacred image had been venerated at Edessa, and in so doing it gives us some hints about the cloth's lodgment. On the day of the icon's major annual festival, the archbishop and other ecclesiastical and political officials gathered in the treasure-chamber, in the Edessan cathedral, in which the icon was regularly kept.

> Then a throne was brought forward, and on it was placed the revered and *acheiropoietos* image of Christ and God, draped with a white linen cloth. Four bishops, if they happened to be present, or otherwise four presbyters, elevated the throne, and holding it aloft they came out from the treasure chamber, the archbishop leading the way.[9]

Obviously, we are dealing here with an object of some size, and not with a small, unframed cloth that the wind could lift and carry. However the cloth was mounted, the icon as a whole was of sufficient bulk that it could be "draped" (the Greek word *perikalyptomenē* literally means "covered all round"), and that, at the high point of the ceremony, the archbishop could "place around" it (*peritithenai*) a cloth of purple. In other words, the Mandylion was a fully three-dimensional object. And just as in Edessa four bishops carried the icon in its annual sacred festival, so in 944, when the sacred cloth first came to Constantinople, the Patriarch Theophylact and the young princes "hoisted it on their shoulders"[10] and carried it to the great church of Haghia Sophia.

We also learn from the "Liturgical Tractate" that in Edessa the icon had been kept in a chest (*thēkē*). In a second annual festival for the icon, the archbishop alone was permitted to enter the room

> and to open the chest in which it was placed, and with a wet sponge that had never been used, to wipe it off and then to dispense to the whole people the drops that could be squeezed out. Anointing their eyes with the drops, they were filled with its sanctifying essence.

In this chest the icon seems to have stood upright. This is implied a few lines further on in the same text:

> And since the old chest was encased with shutters, so that it (i.e., apparently, the icon) would not be visible to all when and whenever they wished, on these two days of the week—I mean on Thursday and Saturday—when these shutters, so to speak, were opened up by means of very slender iron rods that were thrust through (these they called "sceptres"), then all the assembled throng gazed upon it; and every person besought with prayers its incomprehensible power.[11]

In order to stand upright in its shuttered chest, the icon must have been a rigid package. A folded cloth, held snugly against a board, would fit the requirements quite well.

It is theoretically possible that a stout backing board and a slip-covered, three-dimensional frame might have held a rather small and insubstantial cloth, but that is not what the rest of the literary evidence suggests. That *mandylion* means "little handkerchief" is usually, but should not be, taken as establishing that that is what the cloth was. The Latin word *mantīle* (which originally meant "hand-cloth") had by the tenth century been borrowed by several languages in the Near East (today *mandil* is the word for "handkerchief" in Arabic, Turkish, and modern Greek). Whether in Arabic, Syriac, or Greek, the word eventually became the colloquial term for the icon. The Byzantine Greeks attached to *mandil* the diminutive suffix *-ion*, and used the new word as the icon's proper name. It was not a descriptive noun (certainly the Mandylion was not a "little handkerchief") but a colloquial name, perhaps used regularly by the laity, but not by the cloth's official custodians.[12] The name *Mandylion* first appears in a Greek text ca. 990, in a biography of the ascetic Paul of Mt. Latros. The author of the biography says that Paul, without ever leaving Mt. Latros, was granted a miraculous vision of "the icon of Christ not made by hands, which is commonly called 'the holy Mandylion.' " This somewhat condescending reference and two others are the only instances of the name in all the Greek texts in *Christusbilder*.[13]

Formally and properly, the cloth was called "the image not made by human hands"—the *acheiropoietos* icon of Christ.[14] Less formally, it was often called "the imprint"—the *ektypōma* or *ekmageion*. Other authors, noncommittal about its size, refer to the Mandylion simply as a *sindon* ("a linen") or a *hyphasma* ("a woven fabric"). Of the various words in the *Christusbilder* collection that suggest the size of the cloth, some imply that it was a small cloth, like a napkin or towel: Greek authors who refer to the cloth as a *soudarion* ("sweat-cloth") undoubtedly thought of it as rather small, perhaps limited to the cloth exposed to view. Other authors, however, describe it as a large garment. Leon Diaconos, in the late tenth century, called it a *peplos*—a robe.[15] John of Damascus, writing ca. 730, said that Jesus had impressed the image on a *himation*,[16] which was the oblong cloth (almost two yards wide and three yards long) that served as an outer garment for a Greek in antiquity. And the original of the "Latin Abgar Legend," as we shall see, also presumed a cloth several yards long.[17] Where Jesus obtained so much cloth for the miraculous impression was usually not explained. But those authors who do go into the matter say that when Jesus saw that Ananias, King Abgar's emissary, was experiencing difficulty in painting the divine face, Jesus asked for Ananias' own clothes (*vestis, vestimentum*) and thereon imprinted his image.[18]

There is, finally, another reference to the Mandylion as a cloth "folded four times," and so a second instance of the word *tetradiplon* in all of Greek literature. It appears in a document of prime importance in the dissemination of the Abgar legend and the story of the Mandylion. Orthodox congregations in the tenth century listened to appropriate readings on each of the major festivals in the church calendar. The "Monthly Lection" for August 16 was a text that recounted the full history of the Mandylion, for the sacred cloth arrived in Constantinople on August 16, 944.[19] This lection was prepared soon after the icon's arrival, and probably in time for the first anniversary festival. It was composed by the emperor's scholars, who found some of their information in older texts, and some in the memories of "people from Syria." The "Monthly Lection" was something of an official publication, and it provided a basis both for the "Festival Sermon" and for many other, more cursory, versions of the Mandylion's nature and origins. At any rate, in describing the icon's origins, the "Monthly Lection" reports that after Jesus had washed,

> there was given to him a piece of cloth folded four times [*rhakos tetradiplon*]. And after washing, he imprinted on it his undefiled and divine face.

Thus, two literary documents that are fundamental in the evolution and spread of the Mandylion's story—the late sixth-century *Acts of Thaddaeus*, which seems to have been where the story first appeared, and the tenth-century "Monthly Lection"—speak of the icon as a cloth "folded four times." When it was in Edessa and Constantinople, the Mandylion was no more accessible than the Shroud has been in Turin. Most authors who mention the Mandylion could not themselves have approached the icon and touched the cloth, and perhaps many had not even seen it. The two documents that we are here concerned with, on the other hand, are almost canonical in their authority, and their description of the Mandylion must be the basis for any attempt to reconstruct its size and disposition. What exactly the authors meant by a cloth "folded four times" may be debated, but a reasonable guess is that in a slightly expanded form the cloth was arranged something like this:

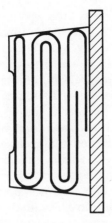

The Mandylion, then, was an ivory-colored linen, bearing a blurred and dim image, the image being described as "not made by human hands" and resembling, in the artists' copies of the Mandylion, the face of the Man of the Shroud. The Mandylion was considerably wider than one would expect as backdrop for a portrait of a face, and was apparently far longer than the height of the exposed cloth. The bulk of the cloth seems to have been folded, in seven folds, behind an exposed, eighth panel. That the seven other folds were nothing but blank linen, carefully concealed but carefully preserved for over a thousand years, is manifestly improbable. If the Shroud does carry, as it seems to, the *vera imago* of Jesus, then what is now known as the Shroud of Turin was in the Middle Ages the Mandylion of Edessa and Constantinople.[20]

* * *

The history of the Mandylion from the sixth century to the beginning of the thirteenth is documented well enough, thanks especially to the "Monthly Lection" and "Festival Sermon," which trace its fortunes from Jesus' miraculous imprinting of it until it came to Constantinople on August 16, 944. Although they describe Jesus' creation of the image and the carrying of the cloth to Edessa, our sources do not have much to say about the sacred cloth before the sixth century. King Abgar and his successor as king of Edessa both worshipped Christ, but Abgar's grandson was a pagan, and in his time the image was hidden away in a vault in the city-wall. There, report the Lection and Sermon, it stayed until it was discovered during the attack on Edessa by Chosroes the Persian, during the reign of Justinian. This attack, which we know took place in 544, was repelled by the Edessans, and the Mandylion was credited with working the miracle that saved the city in that crisis. Not long after, the sacred cloth performed another miracle, at a distance of hundreds of miles. King Chosroes, awed by the power of the Sacred Image that had defeated him, requested that it be sent to him so that it might heal his daughter, who was possessed by an evil spirit. The Edessans were loathe to part with their newly found talisman, and so sent to Chosroes an exact copy. His daughter was cured— so great was the power of the Mandylion that even its copies wrought miracles—and Chosroes sent splendid gifts to Edessa as a token of his gratitude.

The fame of the Sacred Image soon spread, from everywhere pilgrims came to venerate it, and treasures poured into the city of Edessa. Years passed (and, we must note, Edessa fell to the Muslims, a misfortune that our sources pass over in silence). After repeated efforts by the Byzantine emperor to fetch the cloth from Edessa to Constantinople, the transferral occurred in the six thousand, four hundred and fifty-second year from creation (944). In order to acquire the image not made by human hands, Emperor Romanus Lecapenus offered to the emir of Edessa a large payment of silver, the return of two hundred Muslim prisoners taken in an earlier war, and a pledge not to attack the emir's territory again. The Christian subjects of the emir were angered that the Mandylion was to leave their city, even though it was to be taken to the queen of Christian cities, and they attempted in various ways to thwart the transfer. At the Euphrates River a crowd of Edessan Christians vowed that unless God gave them a sign, they would prevent the escorting party from crossing the river. At this, the boat in which the Mandylion had been placed, with no one rowing or towing it and with no winds to assist it, crossed the river on its own, and the Edessans conceded that God wished the Mandylion to adorn the Byzantine capital. All along the route to Constantinople, and especially once within that city's walls, the Mandylion healed the sick, cast out evil spirits, and made the lame walk. It was welcomed in the city with a lavish procession, was placed upon the altar of the great church of Haghia Sophia, where it was worshipped by all the congregation, and was then taken to the emperor's palace, to rest in the Pharos Chapel.

Thus far the Festival Sources. The Mandylion's subsequent history in Constantinople can be pieced together from miscellaneous texts that from time to time mention that it was brought to Haghia Sophia for display, was carried round the city in a procession, or was shown by the emperor to visiting dignitaries. This was the time, the eleventh and twelfth centuries, when artists adorned so many Orthodox churches with paintings of the Mandylion. The face on the Mandylion also inspired the various representations of *Christos Pantokrator*, painted on the domes of churches in Greece, Sicily, Italy and the northern Balkans.[21] Even in France, the cathedral in Laon was sent a painting of the Mandylion in the year 1249. This painting, known as the Sainte Face de Laon, has been assigned to the late twelfth or the early thirteenth century by André Grabar, a distinguished art historian and the first to assess the influence of the Mandylion in Christian art.[22] Beneath the face of Christ the artist placed an inscription, in Old Church Slavonic, which in translation reads "Face of the Lord on the Towel."[23] In the Laon painting, which was done on pine-wood, the towel is still taut and fringed, and the golden trellis-work still appears around the nimbus. We do not know whether the Slavic painter had ever seen the Mandylion itself, but Grabar does point out that paintings of the Mandylion that date from after the early thirteenth century— when the icon disappeared—are quite different from the earlier representations. Painters from the late thirteenth century onward imagined the Mandylion to have been a loosely hanging cloth, and in their representations the horizontal rectangle becomes an upright rectangle, and the gilded trellis vanishes.[24] We are undoubtedly safe in concluding that when the Mandylion was lost early in the thirteenth century, it was still regularly packaged in its embroidered jacket.

It is quite certain, however, that the sacred cloth was not *always* kept in its jacket. Wilson suggests that during the Mandylion's stay at Constantinople someone removed the embroidered case for the first time and discovered that the cloth bore the image not only of Jesus' face, but of his entire body, front and back.[25] The evidence that at least some people knew the full dimensions and contents of the sacred cloth are various. Art historian Kurt Weitzmann years ago observed that in the eleventh century, Christian artists, both in the East and West, for the first time painted *threnos* or "Lamentation" scenes, in which the body of Christ, lying in front of the cross, is the central figure. Around it cluster the weeping women, along with Josesph of Arimathea and Nicodemus. Now Wilson has added the contention that common to all of these Lamentation scenes is a long white cloth, "obviously intended to envelop the body over the head, a cloth we would unhesitatingly identify as a shroud."[26] From the same period there are also, Wilson notes, several references to Jesus' "burial linens" among the relics at Constantinople. One reference even suggests that the *sydoine* or *sindon* which the Byzantines boasted of bore an image. A Frenchman, Robert de Clari, who accompanied the Crusaders to Constantinople in 1204, wrote an account of the amazing relics he saw in that city, and one of these was Jesus' burial shroud. At the church of My Lady St. Mary of Blachernae was

> the Sydoine in which Our Lord had been wrapped, which stood up straight every Friday so that the figure of Our Lord could be plainly seen there.[27]

This linen may have disappeared from Constantinople in 1204. According to de Clari, "no one either Greek or French, ever knew what became of the Sydoine after the city was taken." One may reasonably suppose that this *sydoine*, or *sindon*, was the Shroud, finally being exhibited by the Byzantines as Jesus' burial shroud, and not as a towel on which the living Jesus had impressed his face. A complicating consideration is that the very same de Clari reports having seen the Mandylion, in the Pharos Chapel, in a golden container that was suspended from the ceiling by a silver chain.[28] Wilson therefore concludes that the custodians of the Mandylion, when to their amazement they discovered that it was not a towel but the burial shroud of Jesus, had recourse to deception: they placed a "copy" of the

Mandylion, bearing an image of the sacred face, in the Mandylion's casket, and exhibited the true Mandylion as the burial linen of Christ. It may be, on the other hand, that one and the same cloth saw double duty, being portrayed as Christ's burial shroud at the Friday Mass, but otherwise reposing, as the Mandylion, in the Pharos Chapel. Whichever solution is preferred, Wilson would surely be correct in concluding that from the eleventh century onward the full image was known to the cloth's custodians.

Can we agree, however, that until the eleventh century nobody knew of the full image? Although Wilson supposes that nobody had removed the Mandylion from its gold-embroidered jacket before the eleventh century, it is more likely that all along, even while it was still at Edessa, there were some who knew that the cloth portrayed more than Jesus' face. Undoubtedly the cloth had theoretically always been covered by Abgar's golden trellis, but it must from time to time have been removed in private and unfolded. If even for a century, to say nothing of a thousand years, the icon's custodians had not removed it from its encasing jacket, both the Mandylion itself and its jacket would have been filthy and infested beyond remedy. It is also surprising, if the Shroud had remained folded in precisely the same arrangement for a millenium, that the creases are so dim that they cannot be seen without a photographic enlargement.

One point on which our literary sources leave no ambiguity is that the icon was always kept in secrecy and hedged with mystery, and was seen by the public only at certain times and in specified circumstances. In Edessa, as we have noticed, it was kept within a chest in a guarded chamber: twice a week, when the shutters on the chest were opened, worshippers could gaze upon the icon:

> and every person besought with prayers its incomprehensible power. But nobody was allowed to draw near to it, or to touch their lips or eyes to the holy shape. So holy dread increased their faith, and made them shiver with yet more awe in their worship.[29]

As we have seen, once a year the icon was placed on a throne and was carried in sacred procession to the table atop the altar.

On all other days of the year they refrained from this ritual, because it is not permitted to approach the unapproachable more often, lest by ease of access the bowstring of faith go slack.[30]

In Constantinople the icon was guarded with even more secrecy, kept as it was within the emperor's chapel, and carried in procession only once or twice a century.

Is it conceivable that all of this secrecy—the guarded chamber, the shuttered case, the slip-cover embroidered with gold trellis, the cloth itself folded four times and packed against a board—was perpetuated because no one knew there was anything of interest on the rest of the cloth? To the contrary, it is far more probable that the elaborate precautions were taken precisely because the authorities were under a traditional obligation—the reasons for which had long been forgotten—to keep the cloth's contents a secret from worshippers. Other considerations lead to the same conclusion. As suggested above, one can scarcely imagine that before the eleventh century the cloth had not once been removed from its case, that neither the cloth nor the cover had ever been cleaned, and that the backing board had never been replaced. That the cloth had, in fact, been removed from its encasement during its stay at Edessa is indicated by the documents. In the generally accepted story, as we have seen, Jesus pressed a towel to his face, and ordered Ananias to take the towel, now wondrously imprinted, back to King Abgar. But another version of the story reported that Jesus imprinted not only his face on the cloth, but his entire body. This is the version that we find in the "Latin Abgar Legend." Here we find that in response to the letter that Ananias brought from King Abgar, requesting that Jesus come to Edessa to heal him, Jesus wrote that after he had completed all that the Father had sent him to do, he would send one of his disciples to heal the king.

Si vero corporaliter faciem meam cernere desideras, en tibi dirigo linteum, in quo non solum faciei mee figuram, sed et totius corporis mei statum divinitus transformatum cognosces.[31]

(But if you wish to see my face in the flesh, behold I send to you a linen, on which you will discover not only the features of my face, but a divinely copied configuration of my entire body.)

Having done King Abgar the great honor of writing him a letter, Jesus then honored the king by presenting him with a miraculous image.

> *Nam isdem mediator dei et hominum, ut ipsi regi in omnibus et per omnia satisfaceret, supra quoddam linteum ad instar nivis candidatum toto se corpore stravit, in quo, quod est dictu vel auditu mirabile, ita divinitus transformata est illius dominice faciei figura gloriosa et tocius corporis nobilissima status, ut qui corporaliter in carne dominum venientem minime viderunt, satis eis ad videndum sufficiat transfiguratio facta in linteo. Qui linteus adhuc vetustate temporis permanens incorruptus in Mesopotamia Syrie apud Edissam civitatem in domo maioris ecclesie habetur repositus.*[32]

> (For this same mediator between God and men, in order that in all things and in every way he might satisfy this king [i.e. Abgar], spread out his entire body on a linen cloth that was white as snow. On this cloth, marvelous as it is to see or even hear such a thing, the glorious features of that lordly face, and the majestic form of his whole body were so divinely transferred, that for those who did not see the Lord when he had come in the flesh, this transfiguration on the linen makes it quite possible for them to see. This linen, which until now remains uncorrupted by the passage of time, is kept in Syrian Mesopotamia at the city of Edessa, in a great cathedral.)

This Latin version of the Abgar legend, although possibly translated from a Greek (or Syriac) original as late as the eleventh or even the early twelfth century, reflects a much earlier stage of the legend (von Dobschuetz suggested a date ca. 800).[33] The original from which the Latin translation came was certainly older than the "Monthly Lection," for when the original was composed the cloth was still at Edessa.

The "Latin Abgar Legend" lies behind other and later Latin writers in Western Christendom, among them Ordericus Vitalis, who wrote his *Ecclesiastical History* ca. 1141. To Abgar, according to Ordericus, Jesus sent

> a precious linen, on which he had wiped off the sweat from his face, and on which an image of this same Savior shines forth, miraculously painted: this image shows to whoever looks upon it the appearance and size of the Lord's body.[34]

And Gervase of Tilbury, ca. 1213, also echoed the "Latin Abgar Legend":

> The story is passed down from archives of ancient authority that the Lord prostrated himself with his entire body, on whitest linen, and so by divine power there was impressed on the linen a most beautiful imprint of not only the face, but the entire body of the Lord.[35]

We must suppose, then, that whoever (ca. 800?) composed the document from which the "Latin Abgar Legend" was translated had been told that the cloth bore an imprint of Jesus' entire body. At the time, however, nobody thought of the cloth as a burial shroud. Those who had seen the larger imprint must have been able to believe the very strange story that, in order to satisfy King Abgar's curiosity about his appearance, Jesus had placed his naked body on a large cloth and imprinted upon it his full image. It is not difficult to imagine that the custodians of the cloth might have been perplexed and embarrassed about that full image. In fact, we may be quite certain that if they *had* exhibited the entire cloth, and had had no explanation for it other than that it was Jesus' gift to Abgar, the proprietors of the cloth would not only have encountered utter disbelief, but would have so outraged the public that the cloth would have been destroyed. Especially would this have happened had the display occurred in the great Iconoclastic controversy of the eighth and ninth centuries, when, inspired by the puritanism of their Muslim foes, zealous bands of Christian vigilantes destroyed images of all sorts, and most of the artistic patrimony of Eastern Christendom disappeared. The Iconoclasts looked upon all representations of Jesus as sacrilege, just as most Jews had always been adamantly opposed to any representation of Yahweh. That an image of Jesus' face survived the Iconoclasm in eighth-century Edessa is itself remarkable, and we can only imagine how violently the Iconoclasts would have attacked the Mandylion had they known that it not only portrayed Jesus' body, but portrayed it completely unclothed. Perhaps a cloth portraying the naked body of Jesus would have been preserved had it been explained as his burial shroud. But, given their understanding of the cloth's origins, such an explanation was not yet available to the custodians of the cloth at Edessa. I imagine that once a year two or three of the cathedral's most somber priests were accustomed to service the icon, and that with expressionless faces they removed, cleaned and replaced the cloth.

In Constantinople, after 944, a new interpretation of the "secret" image must have evolved. Those who knew about the full image were still not inclined to exhibit it in public, but there must have been earnest questions about the cloth's real nature: was it indeed a cloth that the living Jesus had sent to Abgar, or was it, as some were suggesting, a cloth in which the dead body of Jesus had been wrapped? Perhaps it was in the tenth or eleventh century that another legend arose, obviously designed to account for a linen thought to exhibit an image of Christ's entire body. The legend appears, among other places, in the *Otia Imperialia* of Gervase of Tilbury:

> When the Lord our redeemer was hanging on the cross, with his clothes stripped from him, Joseph of Arimathea came up and said to Mary the Lord's mother and to the other women who had followed the Lord to his passion: 'Alas, this plight shows how much indeed you loved this righteous man! For though you see him hanging naked on the cross, you have not covered him.' Moved by this rebuke, the Lord's mother and the rest of the women who were with her quickly bought a spotless linen so large and long that it covered the whole body of the crucified Christ. And when the body hanging on the cross was taken down, there appeared imprinted on the linen an effigy of the whole body.[36]

Although this tale was not quite as offensive as the old story that Jesus had prostrated his naked body full length on a cloth for King Abgar's edification, it was not plausible, either. If a cloth had been draped over Jesus' body on the cross, the image would have shown the arms extended, and would have shown only a frontal image. The only satisfactory explanation for the Shroud, surely, was that it was the cloth that covered Jesus' body in the tomb.

That explanation was apparently current, even though it may not have been widely publicized, before the cloth disappeared from Constantinople early in the thirteenth century. The report of Robert de Clari that, in the church of My Lady St. Mary of Blacharnae, he saw "the Sydoine in which our Lord had been wrapped," and that "the figure of our Lord could be plainly seen" on the cloth, does imply that the sacred cloth was being exhibited each Friday as a shroud. These displays, it goes without saying, were not put on for entertainment or instruction, but were part of a solemn mass in one of Constantinople's holiest churches. And they occurred at one of the most desperate moments in Constantinople's history. The Byzantine emperor had always relied on his relics to protect his throne and his city, and in 1204 both were gravely menaced by the Frankish Crusaders. In the event, the relics could not preserve the city or Emperor Alexius IV. The Crusaders breached Constantinople's seemingly impregnable walls, which had withstood sieges by Goths, Saracens and Slavs, and the Byzantine Empire was shattered. As Ian Wilson has suggested,[37] it is reasonable to suppose that the emperor, at the darkest moment in his city's history, resorted to the Shroud as the city's last hope: perhaps Christ would yet save the city, if his burial shroud were at last given the public devotion that was its due. The custodians of the cloth had, I believe, all along known that it held an image of Jesus' body, and for well over a century the image had been interpreted as an imprint from Jesus' crucified corpse. But not until he was threatened with the destruction of his city did the emperor disregard the traditional injunction and reveal the Shroud for public veneration.

*   *   *

Where the Mandylion/Shroud was between the years 1204 and ca. 1355 is not known. Wilson's provocative suggestion is that it became the property of the Knights Templars, and that the "head" that the Templars were accused of worshipping was in fact the face on the cloth.[38] Wilson notes that when the French king executed the two leading Templars in 1314, one was the order's grand master, Jacques de Molay, and the other was Geoffrey de Charnay. Both went to their death insisting that they were innocent of heresy or superstition. It is not too much to suppose that the Geoffrey de Charny who owned the Shroud in the 1350s was of the same family as the Geoffrey de Charnay who was executed in 1314. Wilson speculates that the Templars kept the Shroud in their fortress at Acre, in Palestine, until Acre fell in 1291, and that the Templars brought it to France, along with the rest of their treasures, at the end of the thirteenth century. Some documentary evidence, however, suggests that the Shroud, mounted as it had always been, may have come to France considerably earlier. By 1239 the Latin Byzantine emperor, Baldwin II, was in such dire financial straits that he had not only pawned his son, but had sold his vast collection of relics to Venetian bankers.[39] The collection, which included the Crown of Thorns, was purchased by King Louis IX of France. To secure clear title to the relics, Louis asked their former owner, Baldwin, to issue a public statement conferring them upon Louis. The "Golden Bull" that Baldwin issued itemized the relics, and among them we find what probably was the Mandylion/Shroud: *sanctam toellam tabulae infertam*, "the holy towel, stuffed against a board."[40] Perhaps the Mandylion/Shroud was taken to the Sainte Chapelle in Paris. Or, as von Dobschuetz speculated, it may have never reached Paris. Later inventories of the relics in the Sainte Chapelle, which do mention the pieces of the Cross, the drops of the Holy Blood, and the Crown of Thorns, do not mention a *sancta toella*, and it may be that on its way to Paris the relic was hijacked.[41] (Whatever relics were kept in the Sainte Chapelle were destroyed by the Revolutionaries in 1792.) At any rate, whether in 1239 or, as Wilson prefers, ca. 1300, the sacred cloth must somehow have been brought to France, where it would again come to the world's attention, this time unequivocally as the burial shroud of Jesus.

v / The Edessan Icon

THE Shroud of Turin, if it indeed bears (as it seems to) the direct imprint of Jesus' body, is the same cloth that the Byzantine Greeks commonly called the Mandylion. Before the Mandylion came to Constantinople it was known as the Sacred Icon, or Image, of Edessa. We must now look carefully into that earlier period of the cloth's history, its penultimate phase, as we work our way back to the Apostolic Age and to the crucifixion of Jesus.

When the cloth left Edessa for Constantinople in 944 it had been in the Syrian city for centuries. Christian legend, as we have seen, explained that it had been brought to Edessa by Thaddaeus, or more likely by Ananias, shortly after or shortly before Jesus' death and ascension into heaven. Altogether, therefore, the cloth was supposed to have stayed in Edessa for more than nine hundred years, a period longer by far than its stays in Constantinople and Turin combined.

Ancient Edessa is now the city of Urfa, in southeastern Turkey. Her days of glory are gone, and it is difficult to imagine that this Muslim city was once one of the great cities of Christendom.[1] Its location destined it for a prominent, though temporary, role in history. The city lies east of the upper Euphrates, at the intersection of the northern Mesopotamian valley and the trade routes that crossed from Persia to Antioch and other cities of the Syrian coast. The original name of the city was Urhai, but when Alexander the Great conquered the area the city was renamed Edessa, in honor of a city in Alexander's Macedon (the natives disregarded the new name, and continued to call their city Urhai). The Seleucid Greeks counted Edessa as one of their kingdom's cities until about 130 B.C., when the Seleucids lost control of lands east of the Euphrates, and a native prince proclaimed the city independent. The language of Edessa throughout Seleucid and Roman times was the Syriac variety of Aramaic, that Near Eastern vernacular common to Mesopotamia and to the villages and smaller cities of Syria, Phoenicia, and Judaea. The larger Syrian cities tended, after Alexander's conquest, to be dominated by a Greek-speaking population, and one could also hear Greek in Edessa. But Syriac was the language of both the people and—after 130 B.C.—the rulers.

Edessa's political condition in Roman times was unusual, since the city lay in the no-man's land between the Roman Empire and the Parthian (or, after A.D. 227 the Sassanid) Empire based in Persia. Under native rulers, the Edessans maintained their precarious independence until 239, when the Romans finally abolished the Edessan monarchy and incorporated the city into the Roman province of Osroene. By 239 Edessa was becoming a Christian city, while the Roman emperors and senate regarded Christianity as a pernicious creed, incompatible with Roman values and traditions. In the fourth and fifth centuries, as the Roman Empire (now officially Christian) collapsed and the eastern provinces regrouped around the new, Greek-speaking capital in Constantinople, Edessa was an embattled frontier city of the "Roman" Christians against the Zoroastrian Persians. But it held, protected from the Persians—so the Edessans claimed—by a special blessing that Jesus had communicated to Abgar, in a letter written by the Savior himself. The Syriac dialect of Aramaic maintained itself, the city blossomed with more than a hundred Christian churches, and its legend of invincibility grew through the sixth century. Not that relations between Edessa and Constantinople were ever cordial: the Syrians were not happy living under a Greek regime, and the rapacity of the Byzantine emperors was criticized bitterly. In the ecclesiastical world this quarrel manifested itself in schism: the orthodox "Melkites" had the support of Constantinople, while the Monophysites tended to be hostile to the imperial hierarchy.

In the seventh century the Byzantine Empire lost Edessa to the Arabs, an event that some Monophysite Christians in the city openly welcomed. Thereafter, the official name Edessa lapsed into oblivion, and the place was unanimously Urhai once again. Some citizens began to learn Arabic, a tongue not nearly as foreign as Greek, and the number of Syriac-speakers began to dwindle. Muslim mosques appeared beside the Christian churches and eventually overshadowed them. When the Turks took the city in the twelfth century, Arabic in turn began to give way to Turkish, the name Urhai evolved into Urfa, and the city's Christian traditions came to an end.

Such was the city in which the sacred cloth is reported to have stayed for more than nine hundred years. It must be said at the outset, however, that there is certainty only about the last four of those nine centuries. The whereabouts of the Edessan Icon from the middle of the sixth century onward are in no doubt, but we shall need to establish whether the cloth was worshipped in Edessa before the middle of the sixth century. If we glance over the references to the Edessan Icon in the *Christusbilder* collection, we note immediately that these proliferate in the later centuries and are relatively frequent from about 700 onward. On the other hand, very few authors in earlier centuries have anything to say about the Edessan Icon. The statistics, in fact, point a sharp contrast. From the half-century between 550 and 600 we have two references.[2] Another reference seems to date from the seventh century; and then in the eighth century, when the great Iconoclasm controversy heated up, the number of references mushrooms to fourteen.[3] On the other hand, in the five centuries before 550 there is only one reference to the icon. That reference consists of two sentences in a Syriac text known as *The Doctrine of Addai*,[4] composed some time before 400.

There can be, accordingly, no doubt that the cloth was venerated in Edessa in the eighth century, and even at the very beginning of the eighth century. The absence, or near absence, of seventh-century testimonia to the Edessan Icon is not entirely surprising, since the seventh century was a time of grave difficulty for eastern Christendom: in his *History of the Byzantine Empire*, A. A. Vasiliev observed that "with regard to letters and art, the period from 610 to 717 is the darkest epoch in the entire existence of the Empire. After the abundance of the preceding century, intellectual creativeness seemed to have died out completely."[5]

As far as Edessa itself is concerned, when the city fell first to the Zoroastrian Persians in 609 and then, with finality, to the Muslim Arabs thirty years later, Christian writers would have had little enthusiasm for extolling the icon that was supposed to guarantee the safety of Edessa as a Christian city. However the absence of seventh-century references is to be explained, two Greek texts from the latter half of the sixth century—the anonymous *Acts of Thaddaeus* and Evagrius's *Ecclesiastical History*—leave no doubt that in their time the cloth was in Edessa and was regarded as an *acheiropoietos* icon of Christ. This much is clear: from at least the late sixth century onward the cloth enjoyed its status as the Sacred Image of Edessa.

The many authors who mention the Edessan Icon do not, unfortunately, tell us much about its history. With the exception of Evagrius, who describes the icon's deliverance of the city from Chosroes' siege, writers from the sixth century to the ninth say virtually nothing of the icon's history other than the marvelous episode of Jesus' creation of the image and his sending of the cloth to Abgar. Most of our eighth-century sources on the Edessan Icon mention it briefly—by way of polemic against the image-breakers—as proof that Jesus himself encouraged the use of icons. Neither these authors nor those in the ninth century who mention the Edessan Icon seem to have known much about it except that it was in Edessa, and that it was not made by human hands. When scholars have attempted to reconstruct the early history of the icon—as Sir Steven Runciman did in 1931, and as Ian Wilson has now done[6]—they have perforce relied upon the Festival Sources composed immediately after the icon's 944 arrival in Constantinople. For these sources purport to present a continuous history of the icon, from its miraculous imprinting to the writers' own day.

Even the authors of the Festival Sources, however, were unable to recount more than a very few episodes from the icon's history of almost a thousand years. Neither the substantial "Monthly Lection" nor the still-longer "Festival Sermon" provides us with detail on anything other than three brief seasons in the cloth's history: the reign of Abgar and its aftermath (roughly the generation following A.D. 30), the time of Chosroes (ca. 544–550), and the bringing of the icon to Constantinople (944). The centuries-long intervening periods that separate these three episodes are accounted for in the Festival Sources, but are not described. Let us look at a précis of the longer of these two sources, the "Festival Sermon":[7]

1. Not only God himself, but also many of his works are beyond understanding, yet we must apply ourselves to learn what we can of them, and specifically of this miraculous icon that has now come to the queen of cities.

2. When Jesus was on this earth, Abgar, ruler of Edessa, learned from one of his servants, whose name was Ananias, that Jesus was working miracles in Palestine. Since Abgar suffered from leprosy and arthritis, he sought to learn more about this incredible man.

3–4. Abgar wrote a letter to Christ, asking him to come to Edessa [letter quoted in full].

5. This letter Abgar entrusted to Ananias to take to Christ. Abgar also instructed him that, if he could not persuade Jesus to return with him to Edessa, he should paint Jesus' portrait and bring the portrait back with him. Finding Jesus preaching to a great crowd, Ananias sat on a rock and attempted to draw his portrait.

6–7. Jesus summoned Ananias to him and, in his omniscience, told Ananias what was in the letter. Jesus then gave to Ananias a letter [quoted in full] to take back to Abgar, promising that soon one of the disciples would be sent to Edessa to heal Abgar, and that Edessa would be defended against all its enemies.

8. Christ then washed his face and wiped off the moisture with a towel that was given to him. The likeness of Jesus' face was miraculously transferred to the towel. Christ gave the towel to Ananias, and instructed him to hand it over to Abgar.

8–9. On his way to Edessa, Ananias spent a night in the city of Mabbog, in the yard of a factory where roof-tiles were made, and he hid the cloth under a stack of newly made tiles. During the night there was a great fire, during which the image of Jesus' face on the cloth miraculously copied itself onto one of the tiles. This sacred copy is still today at Mabbog, which the Arabs called Memmich.

10–11. There is another account (less well known, but none-theless possible) of the origin of the image. When Jesus was in the Garden of Gethsemane, and his sweat was, as it were, great drops of blood, he took a cloth and with it wiped off the drops of sweat. "At once the still-visible impression of that divine face was produced." Jesus gave the cloth to Thomas, telling him to give it, in turn, to Thaddaeus, who was to carry it to Abgar. Thaddaeus did so shortly after Jesus ascended into heaven.

12–14. Thaddaeus, arriving at Edessa, healed the sick and so came to Abgar's attention. When Thaddaeus entered Abgar's presence, he placed the icon in front of his own face, and the brightness of the icon dazzled Abgar. Abgar was almost com-pletely healed of his leprosy and arthritis by the cloth. Then Thaddaeus baptized Abgar and his entire family, and Abgar's last remaining spot of leprosy disappeared.

15a. Abgar ordered that the cloth be fastened to a board and be embellished with gold. He placed it above the city's main gate, where had previously stood a statue of a Greek god, and ordered that everyone entering the city worship the miraculous image of Christ.

15b. This worship continued through the reign of Abgar and his son. But Abgar's grandson reverted to the worship of idols and wished to destroy the icon. The bishop, however, knowing the king's wicked plan, walled up the cloth in its niche, above the main gate; before walling it up, the bishop placed a tile above the cloth to protect it, and set a lit votive lamp beside the cloth and the tile. The wicked king, satisfied that the icon was no longer worshipped, relented in his plan to destroy it.

16. "Then a long interval of time elapsed, and the erection of this sacred image and its concealment both disappeared from men's memories." But when Chosroes, king of the Persians, was ravaging the empire's cities, Edessa was in great danger for the Persians had tunneled under the walls and were on the verge of taking the city. Then, Bishop Eulalius saw in the night a vision of a majestic woman, who told him of the icon and its hiding place.

17. At dawn Eulalius found the icon, and with it the votive lamp, still burning, and the tile, on which the cloth had mi-raculously copied itself (this tile is still today in Edessa). With

the lamp and the icon, Eulalius frustrated the efforts of Chosroes and the Persians, and Edessa was saved.

18. This story of the Edessan Icon's deliverance of the city from Chosroes is not an idle tale. Three patriarchs attest to it, as does Evagrius in his *Ecclesiastical History.*

19. Evagrius says that Chosroes constructed a great wall just outside the city's wall, so his soldiers might hurl missiles at the Edessans from a higher position; and when the Edessans were in no other way able to undermine or destroy the Persians' wall, the sacred image helped to light the fire that destroyed the wall.

20. Later, Chosroes himself was aided by the Icon of Edessa. When his daughter was afflicted by an evil spirit, Chosroes asked that the icon be sent to Persia to heal the girl. The Edessans sent him as close a copy as they, with human hands, could make, and the copy drove the evil spirit out of the girl.

21. After Edessa had enjoyed long years of wealth and honor as a result of the icon's presence, it was divinely decreed that the icon should be transferred to Constantinople. So the emperor agreed to surrender, for the icon, 200 Muslim prisoners and 12,000 silver coins . . .

22–30. [In great detail, the transport of the image to Constantinople, and its eventual placement in the Pharos Chapel.]

31. *Prayer to the Icon:* "O Holy Image of the Likeness of the Unchanging Father! O likeness of the likeness of the Person of the Father! O sacred and all-praiseworthy token of the archetypal glory of Christ, our Lord! I speak of you in faith just as if you were alive." etc.

Aside from the devotional chapters with which it opens and closes, the "Festival Sermon" concerns itself with three widely separated episodes in the icon's history. The initial chapters (2–15) recount the icon's miraculous origin, its veneration in the time of King Abgar and his son, and its seclusion in the city-wall during the reign of Abgar's grandson. All this, if we were to translate it into chronological terms, would have to be placed between A.D. 30 and A.D. 60, during the Apostolic Age. The next five centuries, during which time the icon remained concealed in Edessa's wall, our text passes over in a single sentence. Suddenly we find ourselves at the siege of Edessa by Chosroes, which occurred in the year 544. The Sermon's middle section (chaps. 16–20) details the siege and the icon's miraculous deliverance of Edessa from Chosroes' Persians, and tells of one other event in Chosroes' reign. Then we leap forward again, for our text devotes only one sentence to the next four hundred years, remarking that during those centuries the icon brought wealth and fame to Edessa. Finally, the concluding section of the sermon (21–30) describes the transfer of the icon from Edessa to Constantinople in 944. Thus the sermon goes into detail on three brief moments in the icon's long history, and to each of the two vast intervening stretches (lasting five and four centuries respectively) it devotes no more than a sentence. Let us examine this oddly proportioned account of the icon's history.

The last section of the "Festival Sermon" describes several miracles the icon performed en route from Edessa to the Pharos Chapel in Constantinople. These miracles the historian puts to the side, but the sermon's more pedestrian details about the icon's journey to Constantinople are not likely to be too far from the mark. Nor need we doubt the sermon's brief sentence about the four centuries between the reign of Chosroes and 944.

But if we turn to the central section of the "Festival Sermon," we find serious difficulties. We have no reason to doubt that the icon played some role in the Edessans' efforts to thwart Chosroes' siege, although not quite the role that legend assigned to it. But can one accept the story of the rediscovery of the icon by Bishop Eulalius, when the fall of the city seemed imminent? Sir Steven Runciman rejected parts of that story, specifically those tinged with the miraculous: the majestic woman's appearance in a vision, informing Bishop Eulalius of the icon's existence and whereabouts; the lamp still burning after almost five hundred years; the divinely copied image on the tile.

In place of the miraculous events, Runciman proposed a demythologized discovery: during the tunneling operations in 544 the Edessans may have chanced upon some old icon in a wall or a cellar.[8] Miraculous embroidery such as the sermon's is such a commonplace in Byzantine texts that one can normally cut it away while preserving the rest of the story. But here, as

Ian Wilson points out, that procedure will not do. Wilson's objection is that the whole story of a rediscovery in 544 is absent from a much earlier and better source—Evagrius's *Ecclesiastical History*—that celebrates the icon's accomplishments during Chosroes' siege.[9] Evagrius, who lived through Chosroes' invasion of Syria, is in fact cited by the "Festival Sermon" (18–19) as its chief authority for the entire episode, and Evagrius's account implies that the icon was known and available before Chosroes launched his attack. Wilson reasonably concludes that if Evagrius knew nothing about Bishop Eulalius's dramatic rediscovery of the icon, then it is likely that the icon was not rediscovered in 544 but had already become familiar to the Edessans before that date.

Accordingly, Wilson has suggested that the Edessan Icon was found some time before 544. In the year 525, after more than a century of good behavior, the Daisan river that flows through the city leapt its banks and devastated Edessa. According to Procopius of Caesarea, who was not only a contemporary of these events but also a highly reliable historian, the Emperor Justinian himself saw to the repairs of the city, including its walls.[10] Wilson suggests that in the course of these repairs the icon was rediscovered in its niche atop the city's main gate,[11] where, as the sermon says, it had been carefully walled up a few decades after Jesus' passion.

Wilson's reconstruction, alas, is no less vulnerable than Runciman's. Once one rejects, on the basis of Evagrius's silence, the Festival Sources' story of the rediscovery of the icon in 544, one has no reason to suppose that the icon was *ever* rediscovered, for only the Festival Sources speak of a rediscovery. Needless to say, Procopius does not mention it in his account of Justinian's repairs, although the omission need not mean very much, since Procopius was too much of a skeptic to be interested in such things. The same is not true, however, of the authors of the "Edessan Chronicle," a Syriac text composed after 540 and just before Chosroes' invasion.[12] The chronicler was interested in all sorts of ecclesiastical matters, as well as in mundane affairs. The chronicler's entry for 525 describes the flood in detail and how it led to the death of Bishop Asclepius,[13] and then goes on to recount various events of the succeeding years. Had the

Edessans discovered the *acheiropoietos* icon of Christ in one of these years, the chronicler would surely have mentioned it (the chronicler does not pass over in silence the divine fire that in 512 kept Anastasius from placing his menacing hand on an Orthodox text, or the sign of a spear in the sky that was shown to Justinian in 539). That the "Edessan Chronicle" says nothing about the rediscovery of the icon is strong evidence that the icon was not found in the aftermath of the flood of 525.

Let us turn to Evagrius's *Ecclesiastical History* and see precisely what he had to say about the image.[14] This story is one of several that, for Evagrius, demonstrated the continuing miraculous assistance of God to his people. Evagrius says that when Chosroes laid siege to Edessa, the Edessans dug a tunnel to a point underneath Chosroes' colossal siegeworks, and then tried to set the siegeworks afire. Despite all their efforts, the Edessans could not get their fire started:

> When nothing worked, they bring out the god-made icon which was not manufactured by human hands. Christ had sent this to Abgar, when he desired to see him. So this all-holy icon they brought into the tunnel which they had dug; they sponged it with water and with the same water they sprinkled the stack and the timber. And immediately, with divine aid added to their faith, what before had been impossible was now accomplished. For the wood immediately caught fire, and more quickly than one can say it, was burned to ashes and ignited what lay above it.[15]

That is all Evagrius has to say about the Edessan Icon. There is nothing about a rediscovery of the icon during the siege, nor is there any suggestion that it had ever been lost and rediscovered. Evagrius seems to assume that the icon had been there all along, ever since Christ had sent it to Abgar.

Nor does any text earlier than the Festival Sources speak of the icon's concealment and rediscovery, and many imply that the icon had been venerated continuously since its first arrival in Edessa. A Syriac text of ca. 800 states that in Abgar's time "the cloth was brought and, as a source of help, rests until the present day in the church at Urhai."[16] A synodical declaration of three Eastern patriarchs, issued shortly before 836, claims that the holy imprint sent to Abgar has been "up until today" the pride and treasure of Edessa.[17] Another text, aimed at the Iconoclasts and probably dating from the late eighth century, reports that "Christ himself made the image that is called *acheiropoietos,* and until today it still stands and is venerated."[18] John of Damascus writing ca. 730, said that the miraculously imprinted image "has been preserved up to the present time," giving no hint that he had heard a story about its five-century concealment.[19]

If these earlier authors do not seem to doubt that the Edessan Icon had been worshipped without interruption from Abgar's time to their own, why has anyone credited the Festival Sources' story, in however de-mythologized a form, that the icon was rediscovered in the sixth century? The reason is that, with the single exception of the fourth-century *Doctrine of Addai,* no text from before the middle of the sixth century mentions the icon at all. Surely, the argument runs, the icon would not have been so unheralded through all this time if its whereabouts had been continuously known.

There are several fourth- and fifth-century authors in whose works mention of the Edessan Icon is conspicuously missing: Jacob of Serug, for example, and St. Ephraim, both of whom lived much of their lives in Edessa and both of whom were prodigious writers (Jacob produced over 700 pieces of religious poetry).[20] Another whose silence is significant is Egeria, a woman who came from Aquitania on a pilgrimage to Jerusalem and other important Christian sites in Palestine and Syria, apparently in the late fourth century. Her account of what the devout monks and priests showed her in Edessa makes no mention of an *acheiropoietos* icon of Christ, although it does celebrate the letter that Jesus had sent to Abgar.[21] And Eusebius, claiming to base his remarks on the Syriac archives of Edessa, likewise makes much of the correspondence between Jesus and Abgar, but says nothing of the miraculous image.[22] How could these authors have neglected to mention the Edessan Icon, unless during that time the Edessans were unaware of its whereabouts and its very existence?

There is an answer to this question, and for it we need look no further than the one early text that does mention the icon, the Syriac *Doctrine of Addai*. This text was given its final form no later than ca. 400, although its original composition seems to have been considerably earlier.[23] Although this text is mostly about Addai, it begins by describing the mission which Ananias (or, as the Syriac calls him, Hanan) performed for Abgar, and gives the verbatim text of Abgar's letter to Jesus, and of Jesus' response to Abgar. After quoting Jesus' reply, the *Doctrine of Addai* continues as follows:

> When Hanan the archivist saw that Jesus had spoken thus to him, he took and painted the portrait of Jesus with choice pigments, since he was the king's artist, and brought it with him to his lord King Abgar. When King Abgar saw the portrait he received it with great joy and placed it with great honor in one of the buildings of his palaces.[24]

That is all the text tells about the icon, but those brief sentences have an extraordinary significance. In the fourth century, this text shows, the image on the cloth was regarded not as supernatural, but as the product of merely human skill. There lies the explanation for the Edessans' relative indifference to it in these early centuries.

When did the supernatural character of the icon assert itself? As von Dobschuetz argued in meticulous detail,[25] Chosroes' siege of Edessa in 544 was the turning point: the belief that the icon was miraculous arose *as a result of* certain events during the siege. On the other hand, the reconstruction proposed by Ian Wilson reduces the siege to a minor episode in the icon's history. Wilson's analysis is not surprising, since he himself could not believe that the icon had in fact accomplished a miracle that delivered the city from Chrosroes. Such a reconstruction, however, neglects the one and only item in the Edessan Icon's early history that seems to contain a kernel of truth. Somewhere in the events of 544, however distorted the report of them may be in Evagrius's account or in the Festival Sources, occurred the Edessan Icon's great moment. Let us try to appreciate it.

The Sassanid Persians were inveterate enemies of the Byzantine Empire, but whether the war was hot or cold depended largely on the personality and ambitions of the rival leaders, the emperor and the Sassanid king. Chosroes I showed himself to be one of the most aggressive and formidable opponents the empire had ever faced. In 540, breaking a peace treaty that had been signed between the two powers eight years earlier, Chosroes launched a powerful invasion of Syria. He led his army all the way to the Mediterranean, to Antioch, the greatest of Syria's cities, and for the first time in three centuries Antioch was sacked. In the same campaign Chosroes threatened Edessa, but desisted from his attack because of illness. The Edessans attributed his illness to the protective power of Jesus' letter to Abgar. But Chosroes was merely deferring his objective and was said to have been provoked especially by the claim that the Christians' god had made Edessa impregnable. The Persian invaded Byzantine territories again in 544, and this time Edessa was his primary target. The imperial authorities had placed a sizable Byzantine garrison in the city, but the story of the siege is mostly the story of the valor and ingenuity of the citizens of Edessa.

We are fortunate to have a detailed account—about thirteen pages long—of the siege in the *History of the Wars* which Procopius of Caesarea composed in the 550s. Procopius occupied a high position under Justinian at the time of the invasion, and in his later years wrote a masterful history of Justinian's three great wars. His account of the siege of Edessa, which is far and away the best account we have, goes as follows:[26] irritated by the Edessans' faith that Jesus' letter to Abgar had rendered their city immune to capture, Chosroes attacked the city with his full force. After unleashing his mercenary Huns against the city as a foretaste of what was to come, Chosroes summoned negotiators from Edessa and told them that they could save their city by handing over 50,000 pounds of gold. When they heard these impossible terms, the people of Edessa decided to resist to the bitter end, and Chosroes' efforts to reduce the city only intensified their determination. Thereupon, Chosroes conceived a plan to raise, a stone's throw outside the city's walls, a tower-stack so high that from its top the Persian archers would be able to shoot down at the city's wall. The Edessans, when they saw what Chosroes had in mind, tried to set the wooden tower-stack afire with flaming arrows, but these the Persians easily extinguished. Next the Edessans dug a tunnel from within the walls to a point directly underneath the tower-stack. Bringing firewood into it, they tried to start a blaze at the end of the mine, and so to ignite the tower-stack. Although they had difficulty in starting the fire, because of the lack of air in the mine, eventually they succeeded. With these subterranean efforts the Edessans and the Byzantine garrison coordinated a barrage of flaming arrows, so that the Persians on the tower-stack, extinguishing the little fires set by the arrows, for several hours did not suspect that some of the smoke was coming from another and much deeper source. When finally Chosroes himself began to understand that the tower-stack was burning from below, it was too late to do anything. All day the fire gathered strength, and Procopius says that so great was the blaze that the smoke could be seen from as far away as Harran, twenty miles to the south.

Although the construction and destruction of the tower-stack was easily the dramatic climax of the siege, the siege dragged on. Chosroes next tried to scale the walls by night, but was frustrated when a townsman raised the alarm to the citizenry and the Byzantine garrison. The Persians then failed in an attack on one of the gates, and in a general assault, with all of their forces, on a broad stretch of the wall. On this occasion the women of the city shared in the heroics, as they poured hot olive oil on the Persians who were trying to climb ladders set against the wall. Finally discourged, Chosroes agreed to lift the siege in return for a paltry 500 pounds of gold. This the Edessans delivered to him, and the siege ended.

Nowhere in the thirteen pages of his account does Procopius mention the Edessan Icon. Of course, Procopius was not a professional Christian (he was at least a nominal Christian, but by career he was a rhetorician, a secretary to Justinian's great general, Belisarius, and finally an administrator and a senator). Procopius did, however, discuss in some detail, and with some irony, the Edessans' reliance on Jesus' Letter to Abgar;[27] if he had heard it commonly reported that a sacred cloth had been the means of Edessa's deliverance, he undoubtedly would have mentioned the claim, even though he would hardly have endorsed it. Since he spoke Syriac, Procopius would surely have heard the Edessans' own version of the story, and one can only conclude that when he received his information about the siege, the sacred cloth had not yet usurped the major role in the story.

There should be no doubt, however, that the Icon was brought to bear in the crisis of 544. We may suppose that in the emergency, when the Letter of Jesus, read aloud from the main gate, seemed to be offering the city insufficient protection, whatever icons were available were thrown into the breach. It is indeed very likely that, as Evagrius tells us, Abgar's cloth was carried through the tunnel to bless the efforts of those who were attempting to ignite the tower-stack.

In retrospect, after their own valor and ingenuity had been forgotten, the Edessans' recollection was that the cloth had been the city's salvation. In his *Ecclesiastical History* Evagrius shows that other Syrian cities had their own stories about divine aid against Chosroes.[28] The citizens of Apamea insisted that their city was saved when Bishop Thomas was implored by the populace to bring out the wood of the Holy Cross so that all could receive its blessing one last time (Evagrius tells us that he himself—he was then a young schoolboy—was in attendance, having accompanied his parents). As the bishop held the wood aloft and kissed it, a great flame illuminated the entire assembly, clearly predicting that Apamea would be delivered from Chosroes. At Sergiopolis, Evagrius reports, Chosroes' army was intent upon the city's treasures, particularly the bones of St. Sergius. But as they approached the city, the Persians were deceived by a vision of stalwart defenders upon the walls, although in fact the able-bodied men of Sergiopolis had all been drawn off for duty elsewhere, and only young boys and old men remained. If these cities attributed their relatively unspectacular deliverance to divine assistance, it is not surprising that the Edessans, having survived a far more harrowing siege, ultimately gave all glory to whatever icons had been pressed into service.

Although the Letter of Jesus had done its part in the siege, no visible improvement in the Edessans' situation had directly followed its recitation. The image, on the other hand, was remembered as having contributed to their one striking success— the ignition of the tower-stack. From 544 onward, the prestige of the letter began to decline in Edessa, and the icon's began to rise. The creation of the icon was soon attributed not to

Hanan, the secretary of Abgar, but to Christ himself. All along there must have been some in Edessa who questioned whether Hanan had indeed painted the portrait, for the image did not look like other paintings, and some must have supposed that the cloth had been imprinted directly from Christ's face. Their tales about Chosroes' siege convinced the Edessans that the image was a direct and divine imprint, and that Hanan had merely delivered the cloth on which Jesus had miraculously fixed his likeness. The new explanation of the icon's origins was transmitted to other Syrians and Greeks, and eventually to Latin-speaking Europe. It is odd that only the Armenians did not accept the supernatural explanation of the image. Moses of Khorene, writing ca. 700, knew of the high status of the Edessan Icon, but reported that it had been painted by Hanan. And later Armenian writers maintained that opinion.[29]

In the late sixth century, as we shall see, imprinted cloths in five other Eastern cities were acclaimed as *acheiropoietoi* images of Jesus. Entirely ignored before 544, they were glorified in the wake of the Edessan Icon. A trenchant description of the fad can be found in Gibbon's *Decline and Fall*. The Edessans, Gibbon observes, credited the icon with delivering them from Chosroes' siege.

> After this important service, the image of Edessa was preserved with respect and gratitude; and if the Armenians rejected the legend, the more credulous Greeks adored the similitude, which was not the work of any mortal pencil, but the immediate creation of the divine original. The style and sentiments of a Byzantine hymn will declare how far their worship was removed from the grossest idolatry. "How can we with mortal eyes contemplate this image, whose celestial splendour the host of heaven presumes not to behold?" Before the end of the sixth century these images, *made without hands* (in Greek it is a single word) were propagated in the camps and cities in the eastern empire: they were the objects of worship, and the instruments of miracles; and in the hour of danger or tumult, their venerable presence could revive the hope, rekindle the courage, or repress the fury of the Roman legions. Of these pictures . . . the most ambitious aspired from a filial to a fraternal relation with the image of Edessa.[30]

If the fame of the Edessan Icon resulted from the city's survival of Chosroes' siege, it is no cause for surprise that only one text earlier than 544 mentions the icon. Until that time, the icon was generally assumed to be the product of merely human skill, and though it was said to date from the time of Christ, it was not regarded as miraculous. The prolific Jacob of Serug, who died ca. 521, had no reason to say anything about the icon. Jacob was a Monophysite, and the icon seems to have been the property of the Melkites (ca. 700, by which time all Edessans venerated the icon, the Monophysites acquired it by a ruse, but until then the Monophysites' chief treasure was the Letter of Jesus).[31] That a Monophysite would have wished to advertise one of the Melkites' several man-made icons is unlikely. St. Ephraim, too, who died in 373, would hardly have mentioned Hanan's portrait, since he seems not even to have mentioned the letter of Jesus.[32] Nor need we be surprised that Egeria, the pilgrim from Aquitania, did not speak of the icon in her late fourth-century description of the holy places of Edessa. Let us hear her own introduction to that brief description:

> We arrived, in the name of Christ our God, at Edessa; and immediately after our arrival there we hastened to the church and the shrine of Saint Thomas. There, after we had prayed and had done all the things that we customarily did at holy places, we then read, in addition, some passages concerning Saint Thomas. The church there is large and very beautiful and of recent design, and very worthy of being a house of God. Since there were many things that I wished to see, I had to make a three-day stop there. I visited in the city many shrines of martyrs and many holy monks, some living near the shrines, others living far from the city in secluded places where they had their cells.[33]

Three days in Edessa was not a very long time, even for a woman as vigorous as Egeria, and much of that time must have been consumed in reaching the monks' "secluded places" outside the city, and in praying and reading with her hosts. Nonetheless, it is possible that Egeria saw the icon, but found no reason to mention it. Her tour of Edessa occupies a little over four pages in her diary, and half of the account is devoted to the wonderful fishpools that graced the city then, and are still in Urfa today.

(Egeria tells of the pools' miraculous creation, during a Parthian attack on King Abgar: when the Parthians cut off the city's water-supply Abgar read the Letter of Jesus at them, whereupon the sky turned so dark that the enemy could not find the city, and the pools wondrously appeared.) She does not mention the uncorrupted body of St. Thomas, which had motivated her to put Edessa on her itinerary in the first place; nor does Thaddaeus appear in her account, and Thaddaeus was the city's original patron saint. In fact, aside from the fishpools Egeria describes only four of Edessa's attractions: the church of St. Thomas, the old palace of King Abgar, the tombs of Abgar and his family, and the gate through which Ananias had brought the Lord's Letter. Since she mentions no holy statue, and no picture or other representation, it is not at all remarkable that she says nothing about the portrait of Jesus that Hanan had made. In summary: that, with one exception, writers from the third to the early sixth century failed to mention the Edessan icon is not evidence that in their time the icon was "lost." Rather, their failure to mention the icon confirms the conclusion, based on an explicit statement in the *Doctrine of Addai*, that in their time the icon had not yet acquired supernatural standing.

What, then, of the Festival Sources' story about the icon's five-hundred-year concealment and its miraculous rediscovery by Bishop Eulalius? The story appealed, it would seem, for the same reason that it is still valued today: like several recent sindonologists,[34] the Orthodox scholars who concerned themselves with the Edessan Icon's history could in no other way explain how a divinely created icon could have gone uncelebrated for so many centuries. And, unlike today's sindonologists, the Byzantines were not aware of even the single early reference to the icon: the *Doctrine of Addai* was a Syriac text and was apparently never translated into Greek. As far as the authors of the Festival Sources knew, the icon was not mentioned *at all* prior to the sixth century. To explain this silence, a story arose that cannot withstand critical scrutiny. Apart from the supernatural features of Bishop Eulalius's rediscovery of the icon, and apart from the sheer improbability that the cloth and its case could have emerged unspoiled after five hundred years in the wall, what is one to make of the story of the icon's concealment? Abgar had placed the icon above the city's main gate, the Festival Sources report (obviously their authors knew nothing of the statements in the *Doctrine of Addai* that Abgar placed the icon in his palace),[35] but Abgar's grandson reverted from the worship of Christ to the worship of idols, and so decreed that the miracle-working icon should be destroyed. But the then-bishop of Edessa compromised with the king by walling the icon into its niche atop the gate. There it remained, and "the erection of this sacred image and its concealment both disappeared from men's memories."[36] How, one will immediately ask, could a *story* of the icon's concealment have survived from the first century to the sixth, when the *fact* of the concealment had disappeared from men's memories?

A more complete tale attached itself to another cloth, the icon of Cappadocian Caesarea (present-day Keyseri, about a hundred miles southeast of Ankara). Its imprint was advertised as an *acheiropoietos* image of Jesus at least as early as 574:[37] in the little town of Camulia, not far from Caesarea, a woman named Bassa lived during the reign of Diocletian (284–305). Although she wished to be baptized into the Church, her husband, Camulus, who was toparch of the district, persecuted the Christians in conformity with Diocletian's command. Bassa prayed that Christ would give her a sign by appearing to her, and in response to her prayer a divine voice ordered her to place on a table a glass bowl filled with water, and a clean, white cloth. As Bassa knelt outside the room, Jesus appeared at the table, washed his face in the bowl, and dried his face with the cloth. When Bassa inspected the cloth, she found to her amazement that Jesus had miraculously imprinted his image upon it. For the rest of her life Bassa—who now changed her name to Aquilina—treasured the cloth. But as she neared the end of her life, she decided that she must preserve the cloth from the enemies of the Church. Accordingly, Aquilina wrote out the full story of the image and sealed up the story, along with the cloth itself, a thurible of incense, and a lighted votive lamp, in the exterior wall of her house. Many years later, in the days of the Christian emperor Theodosius the Great (378–395), Bishop Gregory of Nyssa (the most famous bishop the area produced) was moved by the Holy Spirit to open the wall. There he found the cloth, the account that Aquilina had written, the thurible with its incense, and the votive lamp, still burning. He fetched the cloth with its *acheiropoietos* image to the metropolis, Caesarea, where it performed many miracles of healing.

This story of the Caesarea icon, which so closely parallels the Festival Sources' story of the Edessan Icon's concealment and rediscovery, was composed before 787, since it was quoted at an Ecumenical Council in that year.[38] Perhaps it arose during the eighth century in the struggle against the Iconoclasm: that Aquilina's votive lamp kept burning for almost a century was a powerful illustration that God himself saw to it that a venerable icon was continuously honored. The story of the Edessan Icon's concealment may have arisen for the same reason and during the same period, and surely the two stories were related (the text that has come down to us on the Caesarean icon was, like the "Monthly Lection" on the Edessan Icon, included in the corpus of readings for the Orthodox church-year).[39] We cannot establish which of the two stories of concealment and rediscovery was the older, but the Caesarean story was undoubtedly less defective in its structure: Aquilina placed a written account of her cloth in the secret chamber, and so the account was preserved for Bishop Gregory to find and read. The authors of the story in the "Monthly Lection" neglected this crucial detail.

The Festival Sources' story of the Edessan Icon's five-hundred-year imprisonment atop Edessa's main gate, it seems, is a fairly late legend. Although probably a product of the Iconoclasm, it is not attested before 944. Nor is it compatible with the apparent assumption of earlier authors that the icon had been worshipped without interruption since Abgar's time. Because the story was elaborated in ignorance of the *Doctrine of Addai*, it is likely to have developed in Greek rather than in Syriac circles (von Dobschuetz made the pertinent observation that the hero of the story, Bishop Eulalius, has a Greek name, while according to Syriac sources the bishop of Edessa in 544 was Jacob bar Addai).[40] The story of the concealment and rediscovery of the Edessan Icon, we may conclude, is no less legendary, and no more reliable as an historical source, than the story of Jesus' miraculous imprinting of it as a gift for Abgar.

* * *

Finally, we shall need to determine, as best we can, when the Edessan Icon arrived in Edessa. Once again, it would be naive to accept without examination what was said on the subject by an ancient or medieval writer. One can trace a story's evolution, and perhaps can even discover the "original" form of the story, but having done so one cannot assume that the story is history.

The earliest reference to the icon at Edessa is the brief statement in the Syriac *Doctrine of Addai:* after Christ had given his response to King Abgar's letter, the courier Ananias painted Jesus' portrait and brought it back to King Abgar, who was much pleased with it and kept it in his palace. From this account we can conclude nothing more than that when the *Doctrine of Addai* was given its final form (apparently ca. 400), the "portrait" was known in Edessa. In an earlier form of the Syriac text, known to Eusebius at the beginning of the fourth century and probably composed in the late third century, the "portrait" was apparently not mentioned. Eusebius found in this Syriac text, and translated into Greek for his *History of the Church,* the full story of Abgar's correspondence with Jesus, including the complete texts of the letters the two exchanged.[41] For both Eusebius and his Greek readers all of this was new and surprising, but since the Syriac text claimed (falsely) to be based on "the royal archives of Edessa," Eusebius accepted the story and vouched for its reliability. With Eusebius's authority behind it, the story soon spread through all the Christian Church and remained popular for centuries. For our purposes, however, the important point is that the third-century prototype of the *Doctrine of Addai,* unlike the version of ca. 400, may not have mentioned Hanan's painting of Jesus' portrait. In the Syriac text that Eusebius translated, the story of Abgar and Jesus was in point-for-point (and in many places in word-for-word) agreement with the later Syriac text.[42] The absence of the two sentences about the portrait in Eusebius's translation is thus quite conspicuous. Some scholars have supposed that the third-century Syriac text did mention the portrait, but that Eusebius chose to suppress it because of his belief that possession of any image or portrait of Jesus was idolatrous.[43] That solution, however, has some difficulties. Certainly Eusebius was opposed to icons and images of all kinds. But Eusebius was also convinced that what the Syriac text said about Abgar and Jesus was true, and if that text had declared that Jesus permitted his picture to be painted by Abgar's courier, Eusebius would most likely have done one of two things: he might either have attacked that part of the story as a wicked lie, or he might have concluded that his antipathy to icons was wrong, because Jesus himself had sanctioned their use. Eusebius, however, went to his grave confident that icons were un-Christian, and in none of his polemic on the subject is there any sign that he had heard the story of Hanan's portrait. It is likely, therefore, that the sentences about the "portrait" were added to the evolving *Doctrine of Addai* some time between Eusebius's day and ca. 400.

That the reference to Hanan's portrait may have been inserted into the *Doctrine of Addai* around the middle of the fourth century would not mean that the cloth came to Edessa at that relatively late date. Even ca. 400 the "portrait" was given only a brief and modest mention. Perhaps a century earlier the Christians of Edessa paid it even less attention. And perhaps the icon was mentioned in other, now-lost Syriac texts of the third century. Silence about the icon in Christian writers earlier than the fourth century does not establish that the cloth did not come to Edessa until the fourth century.

Legend claimed, of course, that the cloth had come to Edessa around the time of Jesus' ministry or ascension. In the earliest form of the legend known to us, the image was painted by Ananias, the courier, when he delivered the letters of Abgar and Jesus. In the second form of the legend, which arose after the dramatic events of 544, Ananias tried but failed to paint Christ's portrait, and Jesus himself then imprinted his face on the cloth. When Ananias brought the miraculously imprinted cloth to King Abgar, the sixth-century *Acts of Thaddaeus* declared, the king was healed of his dread disease (the earlier understanding had been that Thaddaeus/Addai had healed the king but once the cloth was regarded as supernatural, it usurped Thaddaeus' role).[44] The third form of the story, popular after the icon was moved to Constantinople in the tenth century, held that the person who brought the cloth to Edessa was not Ananias but

Thaddaeus, and that it had been imprinted by Jesus during his agony at Gethsemane.[45]

None of the successive versions of the legend is usable as history. If the Edessan Icon was the Shroud, as we are here assuming, then none of the stories reflect any knowledge of what was actually on the cloth, or how it was imprinted. In an indirect way, however, the legends do tell us something. When the final version of the *Doctrine of Addai* was composed ca. 400, the cloth must already have been in Edessa long enough that the Christians of that city could *believe* that it had been there since before Jesus' passion: it had, that is, arrived in Edessa so long before 400 that the memory of its arrival had disappeared. This suggests a lapse of at least several generations, and pushes the icon's arrival back toward the third century.

Perhaps we can go still further. In the earliest form of the legend the "portrait" was painted by King Abgar's courier, and was placed in the king's palace. This association with the king is curious. For Christians in the fourth century the story would have done more honor to the cloth by assigning its creation to one of the Twelve Apostles, or to some other New Testament figure, rather than to one of King Abgar's underlings. And that this unique portrait should have been kept in the palace, as an *objet d'art*, would probably also have demeaned it in the eyes of a late fourth-century Christian (much later, as we have seen, the Byzantines claimed that Abgar set it atop his city's main gate, where it was worshipped by all the populace). The fact that what little the *Doctrine of Addai* has to say about the "portrait" relates it to the monarchy can most easily be explained as a memory of an historic fact. The Edessan monarchy lasted until the early third century: effectively it ended in 214, when the Romans made Edessa a Roman *colonia* and canceled the city's independence, although a shadowy, titular "king" remained on the scene until ca. 239. It may well be that until the monarchy's end the royal palace was the place where the cloth, packaged in its expensive gilded jacket, was kept. How the Edessan monarchy had obtained the portrait would in that case have required an explanation, and perhaps it was to fill that need that the story arose of Ananias' painting Jesus' portrait.

If the cloth did at some time enter the Edessan palace, it perhaps did so during the reign of Abgar IX, Abgar the Great, who ruled from 177 to 212. Although Abgar the Great was not himself a Christian, he seems to have been a patron of Julius Africanus, the first Christian chronographer, and was a friend of several prominent poets and philosophers on the fringe of the Christian movement.[46] There is, on the other hand, no evidence that any of Abgar the Great's predecessors was sympathetic to Christianity. Legend claimed that Abgar V, Jesus' contemporary, was converted to Christianity along with his entire city, but the legend has no support. Neither the New Testament (here one looks especially in Acts and Revelation) nor any second-century Christian writer says anything about Christians at Edessa, much less about a Christian king there. The evidence of the city's coins, inscriptions, and cults suggests that Edessa remained an essentially pagan city until at least the end of the second century.[47] And finally, Bishop Serapion of Antioch, whom the *Doctrine of Addai* regarded as roughly contemporary with the conversion of Edessa, is from reliable sources known to have been bishop in Antioch ca. 190.[48] There is no likelihood at all that Abgar V received the "portrait" in the time of Jesus himself.

To conclude this history of the Edessan Icon: the icon was there to be seen in Edessa for centuries before 544, but before the climactic events of that year it was not regarded as divine, either in its protective power or in its origins. As "Hanan's portrait of Christ" by A.D. 400 it had been prized and admired, but not venerated, for at least several generations. Possibly the cloth was placed in the royal palace of Edessa toward the end of the second century, in the reign of Abgar the Great. Beyond that, our Edessan sources cannot take us.

vi / *The* Forma Christi

THE Christian artistic tradition is so vast, and of such sur- passing quality, that one can easily forget that Christianity needed almost a thousand years to come to terms with repre- sentational art. From the mosaics of San Vitale in Ravenna to the masterpieces of Michelangelo and Raphael, Christian art represents one of the most sublime products of mankind's creative spirit. Yet in the first and second centuries, Christians looked upon art of all kinds as incompatible with the true religion, and in the eighth and ninth centuries the Eastern Christian world suffered through a violent onslaught against represen- tational art, and most of the Byzantine empire's artistic inheritance of the time was destroyed.

The early Church seems to have been resolutely opposed to icons, whether sculpted or painted. The Jews had traditionally nursed a singular antipathy to graven images, and distinguished themselves from gentiles by their insistence that their god could not be portrayed in visible form. Whereas the Egyptians, As- syrians, Phoenicians, Greeks, and Romans could not conceive of a deity without a statue, the Jews regarded it as sacrilege to portray Yahweh in any material medium. In fact, for the Jews it was axiomatic that a god who *could* be reduced to an image was by definition not a god at all: idolatry means, etymologically, "worship of an image." So strong was this aversion to rendering deity in visible form that most Jews condemned representational art altogether: although there are a few notable exceptions, the Jews in ancient times did not portray the human face or figure, whether in picture or statue.[1] The early Christian Church inherited this hostility to images and regarded them as quintessentially pagan. The Christians of the first two centuries seem to have worshipped God the Father and God the Son in a purely spiritual manner, while "the Greeks" brought sacrifices to cult statues and delighted in pictures of their gods and goddesses. Some Christian churches proscribed not only art but also artists, listing the latter along with drunkards, prostitutes, athletes, and actors as persons who could have no part in the Christian communion. This attitude was tempered slightly in the third century, but was not substantially changed until long after Christianity became the Emperor's religion. Even in the late fourth century Epiphanius, a bishop from Cyprus, cut down an image he found in a church in the little Palestinian town of Anablatha. Although the image represented Christ or a saint (Epiphanius was not sure about the details), the bishop declared that "the authority of the Scriptures" forbade the presence of such a thing in a church.[2] Similarly, when Eusebius chanced upon a woman carrying images of Peter and Paul, he took them from her, lest she be the cause of scandal to other Christians.[3] Evidently, the laity in particular drifted toward images and representational art, while bishops and theologians attempted to keep the Church free of icons. A moderate amount of Christian art has been found in the third-century catacombs in Rome, but at present the only known third-century Christian paintings in an above-ground structure are frescoes found in a house in the Mesopotamian city of Dura-Europus.[4]

With the Edict of Milan in 313, which gave to Christians the Emperor's guarantee that they would no longer be persecuted, a slow shift began in the Church's attitude toward the arts: the construction of large and imposing basilicas was soon followed by the production of specifically Christian mosaics, frescoes, and statuary. By the fifth century Christians had adopted many of the practices that their predecessors had so vehemently denounced as pagan: images of Jesus, Mary, the Apostles, and saints were prominently displayed in churches, where worshippers burned incense and lit votive lamps before them, and wreathed them with garlands. The custom continued unchecked until the eighth century, when the violent reaction known as Iconoclasm occurred. For more than a century militant Christians tried to purify the Church of images, and easterners of three religions outdid each other in puritanical zeal (Islam set the example of a creed without icons, and Judaism, too, tried to rid itself of the graven images that it had begun to countenance in late antiquity). Iconoclasm waned in the ninth century, and thereafter in the Eastern church, as in the Western, representational art was important in focusing and encouraging worship.

Since Christians were by and large opposed to images in the first two centuries, they evidently had no "conventional" image of Jesus during that time. Christian art from that early period has not survived, and for all that we know Christian representational art may not have begun until the third century. Even if it is granted (as perhaps it will be) that Christians of the first two centuries must have produced *some* representational art, it is very unlikely that they painted portraits or sculpted statues of Jesus. Early Christian writers indicate that Christian communities possessed no such images of their Lord.[5]

In the early third century the sepulchral art of the Christian catacombs in Rome begins. Here we find representations of the Good Shepherd, a beardless youth carrying a lamb on his shoulders. This figure, of course, represented Jesus, although it is not clear that third-century Christians supposed that Jesus looked like the beardless youth. They may out of reverence have presented him in the idealized form of the Young Man, a Classical image that had served to portray many outstanding persons, human and divine, from Olympic athletes to Apollo and Hermes. In the proliferation of Christian art in the fourth century, we find that most artists continued to present Christ as a beardless, idealized youth. This is the figure we see most often, not only in the symbolic scenes of the Good Shepherd, but also in the narrative scenes of Jesus performing a miracle or teaching his disciples.[6] (See Plate 6.)

In sharp contrast to this Classical or Hellenic figure, there appears now and then in these early years the un-Hellenic face that has for fifteen centuries been the "conventional" face of Jesus (see Plate 7). In these occasional representations, Jesus is not an idealized youth, but a long-haired, bearded, mature man, with a face less broad than that of the typical Hellenic youth. Some art historians and students of early Christianity have suggested that this bearded figure symbolized Jesus as philosopher or teacher, and was therefore just as much a stereotype as the Classical Youth. For several reasons, however, that suggestion is not persuasive. In the third and fourth centuries there seems to have been no such artistic stereotype, and even if there had been, it is uncertain that Christians would have wished to enroll Jesus in that company.

The interpretation of the bearded figure of Jesus as a symbol of the philosopher has been proposed mostly because no other explanation for the bearded figure has been available. Nor has it seemed possible that the bearded figure might have been an attempt at authentic portraiture, because the Church Fathers, from Justin Martyr in the second century to Augustine at the beginning of the fifth, seem to have been ignorant of any tradition of supposedly authentic portraits. According to Augustine, for example, no one knew what Mary, the disciples, or other figures in the Gospels looked like, and even "the face of the Lord himself, whatever it was," was portrayed in many different ways by different artists.[7] When confronting Celsus's slander that Jesus was short and ugly, Origen in 249 relied entirely on the testimony of Old Testament passages that he interpreted as prophecies of Jesus. "Admittedly," he said, "it is written that the body of Jesus was ugly, but not, as he [i.e., Celsus] asserted, that it was also undistinguished; nor is there any clear indication that he was little."[8] On the basis of the Patristic writings, many scholars from von Dobschuetz to the present have quite reasonably assumed that third- and fourth-century Christians did not have access to any portrait-tradition claiming to represent Jesus' features authentically.[9]

Those assumptions are now upset by the Shroud. If the Shroud bears the direct image of Jesus' body (and a carbon test may leave no realistic alternative), then, despite the early Church Fathers, the occasional third- and fourth-century representations of a long-haired, bearded Jesus not only were intended to be, but in fact *were* realistic portraits of Christ. Six of these "authentic" representations have survived from Roman art of the third and fourth centuries: the earliest, from the Tomb of the Aurelii, was painted ca. 250 or slightly earlier, and the other five date from the fourth century. After 400, the "authentic" representation comes to the fore in the eastern empire, although in the west Jesus was occasionally portrayed as the Classical Youth as late as the seventh century.[10] (See Plate 9.)

The question now arises, how was the "authentic" portrait of Christ preserved and disseminated before 250? As "Hanan's Portrait of Christ," the Shroud was perhaps in Edessa in the fourth century, and would apparently have come to that city before the end of the second century. Indirectly it may have been the Shroud—although undoubtedly packaged in its frame, with only the face visible—that inspired the Roman portraits, but obviously the Shroud itself was not in Rome in the third and fourth centuries. The reasonable answer to the question is that at a fairly early date, and certainly before 250, artists had painted "authentic" portraits of Jesus, portraits that either were modeled on the face on the Shroud, or came down in a tradition parallel to the Shroud. These "authentic" portraits must have proliferated and traveled westward to Rome. And yet, Christian writers show that the early Christian Church had no tradition of "authentic" portraiture of Jesus.

But others did. The Christian apologist Irenaeus (who was born in Asia Minor, and who in 177 became bishop of the Christians in the Gallic city of Lugdunum) charges that portraits of Christ, which were supposed to be in the tradition of an authentic—though not a miraculous—image made when Jesus was still among men, were kept by a group of the Christians' Gnostic rivals: the Carpocratians.[11] A few other Christian writers echo this charge, but Irenaeus's own statement is crucial, for it shows that the Carpocratian Gnostics not only had portraits of Jesus in the second century, at a time when Christians themselves had not yet begun to portray Christ, but also that these Gnostics supposed their portraits to be authentic, when Christian apologists claimed no knowledge of the physical appearance of Jesus.

In proportion to their significance in the ancient world, far too little is known about the Gnostics. During the second and third centuries, Gnostics were found in many cities of the Roman Empire and in Mesopotamia, and their beliefs had a broad impact on several religious cults and philosophical schools. Gnosticism seems to have competed especially with Christianity, however, and according to Christian tradition the competition began as early as the time of Peter and Paul. Irenaeus, in his denunciation of the Gnostics, identifies Simon Magus, the Samaritan magician who tried to buy the Holy Spirit from Peter, as the perpetrator of Gnosticism, although, according to Irenaeus, Satan himself was the originator of the system. Another Christian writer of the second century, Hegesippus, claimed that Gnosticism arose in Judaea at the death of James the Righteous, the Lord's brother: when the Church elected Symeon, one of Jesus' cousins, as James's successor, a disgruntled would-be bishop named Thebuthis defiled the hitherto-virgin Church with Gnostic error. At whatever point their bitter quarrel with Gnosticism began, once they gained control of the police power of the empire (in Constantine's reign), the Christians persecuted Gnostics wherever they found them. Gnostic writings were systematically destroyed, and by the end of the fifth century the "heresy" was finally eradicated. So successful was the Christian suppression that when, in the eighteenth century, scholars became curious about the mysterious and Satanic heresy that so many of the Church Fathers had attacked, not a single Gnostic text was known, and scholars had to content themselves with the polemical statements of Irenaeus and his successors.[12]

Today the situation is somewhat different. As the fourth-century persecutions intensified, Gnostics seem to have hidden away their texts. Although everywhere else the texts would have disintegrated, in the sands of Egypt a number survived until the present day. A few were discovered before the twentieth century, but by far the most important collection of Gnostic texts was found by an Egyptian peasant in 1945, near the town of Nag Hammadi, north of Luxor. Only within the last few years have translations of these fifty-three Coptic texts appeared, and it is safe to say that in the years ahead a much better understanding of Gnosticism will emerge.[13] In the meantime, tentative generalizations will have to suffice.

Unlike orthodox Christianity, which was in large part unified by the year 200, Gnosticism was never brought under a single authority, whether a canon of scriptures, a creed, or an episcopal hierarchy. As a result, Gnosticism was not a church at all or even a philosophical school, but an ill-defined and continually splintering spiritual movement. Eventually there were several major varieties of Gnosticism—Basilidian, Marcionite, Carpocratian, Valentinian—along with infinite minor variations, but all of them were centered on *gnosis*, "knowledge." Knowledge, for them, began with acceptance of one fundamental teaching: man is a spiritual being, trapped in a physical body.

A dualism of this kind, which regards the material world as evil and identifies good with another and spiritual world, was not uncommon in antiquity. Plato taught something approaching this (although for him the antitheses were not so much good and evil as real and unreal) in the fourth century B.C., and centuries earlier in Persia the "Zoroastrian" religion was essentially dualistic. Since Gnosticism was vaguely akin to these and other dualistic systems, scholars have been uncertain where and when Gnosticism began. The traditional explanation had been that Gnosticism began in the first century as an heretical movement within Christianity, and that it then branched into a variety of sects, a few of which had almost nothing in common with Christianity. Eighty years ago some scholars proposed, as an alternative explanation, that Gnosticism arose before Christianity, in Hellenistic or Iranian circles, and that it was merely influenced by Christianity (especially the latter's emphasis upon Christ as the world's savior). The effort to trace Gnosticism to Iranian or Greek roots, however, has now been largely abandoned. Publication of the Dead Sea Scrolls, and more recently of the Nag Hammadi texts, has thrown a floodlight on heterodox (or heretical) Judaism during the late Hellenistic and Roman periods, and it is now apparent that Gnosticism arose as a Jewish heresy. The Dead Sea Scrolls show that a dualism of "light and darkness" was fundamental to the Essene community at Qumran. Perhaps this dualism was remotely inspired by Zoroastrian teachings, but clearly it was flourishing in Judaea itself before the birth of Christ. As for the Nag Hammadi texts, they suggest that their Gnostic authors must have come out of a Jewish tradition: not only are these authors thoroughly conversant with the Old Testament, but in reinterpreting it or attacking it they use exegetical methods that were perfected in rabbinic schools.

Although historians have lately discovered that Gnosticism was rooted in Jewish heterodoxy, and are agreed that it arose in the first century, there is not yet a consensus about the circumstances in which it began. Some scholars are inclined to look for its origins in the early decades of the first century. Like the Dead Sea Scrolls, the writings of Philo of Alexandria (born ca. 30 B.C.) show that by the time of Christ there were already tendencies in Jewish thought that seem to anticipate Gnosticism. On a different level, vaguely Gnostic teachings and practices perhaps were to be found among the followers of John the Baptist (there was a tradition that Simon Magus inherited the thirty disciples of John). Other scholars, especially R. M. Grant, have suggested that Gnosticism arose toward the end of the first century: the apocalyptic expectations of many Jews were dashed in the disastrous rebellion against Rome that began in A.D. 66, and which culminated with the Romans' capture of Jerusalem and burning of the Temple in 70, and Gnosticism arose out of this bitter disappointment.[14]

At any rate, as it appears in the second and third centuries, Gnosticism was laden with Jewish terminology and presuppositions, while at the same time it represented a radical reaction to, or a break with, the central dogmas of the Jewish religious tradition. According to the Gnostics, the god who created the world was Yaldabaoth, but neither the god nor his creation, over which he still rules, is good. The world of the spirit, however, is perfect, and that world is ruled by a deity whom the Gnostics usually called the Father. Disappointed as they were with the physical world, the Gnostics pinned their hopes on the soul, which they believed to be immortal (apocalyptic Judaism had not recognized a soul, nor any existence apart from the body). At death, the Gnostic's soul was thought to leave the evil Emptiness over which Yaldabaoth presides, and to join the Fullness of the Father. In his *Gnosticism and Early Christianity*, R. M. Grant concluded that Gnosticism was "essentially self-knowledge, recognition of the divine element which constitutes the true self."[15] It must be added, however, that although this profound doctrine was somewhere near the core of Gnosticism, it became enmeshed in an almost impenetrable overgrowth of mystical and mythological rubbish: mystical numbers, aeons, powers, demons, the Seven Archons, the 365 angels, exotic Egyptoid names—Barroph, Ibikan, Evanthen, Phthave, Sostrapal—and on and on.

Their "secret teachings," most Gnostics claimed, had been revealed to the wise by the aeon Jesus, whose soul was, as it were, a messenger from the spiritual world of the Father to the material world. For the Gnostics Jesus was not God, was not born of a virgin, and was not a worker of miracles (although given to magic, the Gnostics made less of miracles generally than did the Christians), but a divine teacher, the Son of God in a spiritual sense, and the source of true wisdom. The Gnostics knew and frequently cited the Christian Gospels and the letters of Paul, but in addition to these texts they had other books that were supposed to contain the teachings of Jesus. Among them one can find *The Gospel of Philip, The Gospel of Thomas, The Apocryphon of John, The Sophia of Jesus Christ, The Gospel of Mary*, and many more. Although the manuscripts that have been discovered are all Coptic translations of the fourth century, many of the texts were composed—in Aramaic, Syriac, or Greek— considerably earlier, some of them in the second century and perhaps a few even in the first. In the main, however, specifically Gnostic literature appeared later than (and perhaps its composition was stimulated by) Paul's letters and the Synoptic Gospels.

The early Christians looked upon the Gnostics as their most dangerous adversaries, precisely because the Gnostics claimed Jesus as one of their own and ascribed to him doctrines that orthodox Christians deplored and rejected. According to the Gnostics, Jesus was above all a teacher, and the essence of his teaching was that man's real self is the soul. And Jesus himself has proved that his teaching was true, said the Gnostics, because after his bodily death his spirit, as a luminous presence, has appeared to those who have accepted the *gnosis* that he brought to the world. The Gnostic version of Jesus' teachings, and of his soul's conquest of death, was apparently preached even before the New Testament was written.[16] In the Letters of John and in Paul's letters to the Colossians and to the Corinthians, there are passages that seem to be directed at Gnostic, or proto-Gnostic, followers of Christ. The Second Letter to Timothy (2 : 17–18) accuses two men, Hymenaeus and Philetus, of preaching a spiritual, rather than a physical, resurrection, and this doctrine is the subject of one of the Nag Hammadi texts, the

Treatise on Resurrection.[17] The Christians, like the Pharisees, believed in a physical resurrection and a judgment at the end of the world.

Although it began in the first century, Gnosticism had its heyday in the second and third centuries, after which it receded drastically. In its time it was highly attractive, appealing—with its odd mixture of the profound, the exotic, and the absurd— to educated but disaffected men and women of many nations: Jews, Greeks, Romans, Syrians, Egyptians, and even Parthians. Because of its emphasis on secret wisdom, however, Gnosticism was always exclusive and elitist, and was incapable of the mass conversions frequently accomplished by Christianity. The latter required simple belief in a series of miraculous events that were said to have occurred on this earth. Gnosticism, on the other hand, required the comprehension of a mystical and fantastic otherworld. In the end, Gnosticism was too precarious a move- ment to survive, but its influence is still with us.

Gnosticism and Christianity, it is thus beginning to appear, may have been siblings, both sprung from the same Jewish background, although Christianity saw itself as a continuation and fulfillment of the Old Covenant, while Gnosticism openly renounced the traditional worship of Yahweh. Is it perhaps possible that one of the formative events in the rise of Gnosticism was the teaching and passion of Jesus, though Christians and Gnostics disagreed profoundly on the nature of his person and teaching? What is the likelihood that the Gnostics, rather than the Christians, were the original custodians of the Shroud? The Shroud has for so long been associated with Christianity that most of us have assumed that the Christians could have been the only group that had any interest in it. But in the second and third centuries the Gnostics would have been far more likely than the Christians to have preserved and valued the Shroud.

The earliest known representation of Jesus as a bearded, long- haired man, we have noted, appears in Rome: not, however, in the catacombs, but in the Tomb of the Aurelii (see Plate 5). This elaborate underground structure, which was discovered in 1919 beneath the intersection of the Viale Manzone and the Via Luigi Luzzatti (near the Stazione Termini), dates from the first half of the third century.[18] When the Aurelii, obviously a fairly wealthy family, excavated their hypogeum, it lay outside the walls of Rome (burial within the city's walls was not permitted). But when a new wall was begun on a new circuit in 270, and the Tomb of the Aurelii was suddenly within the city's walls, the tomb had already been in use for several decades. The hypogeum consists of several rooms, all of them painted. Although the paintings contain some Christian elements (the room with the bearded Christ was devoted entirely to the theme of the Good Shepherd), most art historians have concluded that the Aurelii were not orthodox Christians. In the words of André Grabar, "the decoration of this tomb is . . . a work of some complexity: not painted for a Christian milieu, it nonetheless includes some Christian themes."[19] Offering an explanation for this tomb and its paintings, so different from the catacombs of the Christians, Grabar suggests that "it may be that the artists employed by the Aurelii invented their Christian imagery *ad hoc*, suiting it to the taste of Gnostic patrons—which would also explain the absence of images of this type in normal Early Christian Art."[20] It is not *known* that the Aurelii were Gnostics, but they do seem to have been a para-Christian family, and in the first half of the third century there were a good many Gnostics in Rome. This, then, is a small piece of evidence that the representation of Jesus as a long-haired, bearded man might have been introduced to Rome in Gnostic circles. The earliest such representations in purely Christian contexts—a fresco in the Catacomb of Commodilla and two mosaics in the church of S. Costanza—date from about the middle of the fourth century, more than a hundred years later than the bearded Good Shepherd in the Tomb of the Aurelii[21] (see Plates 7 and 8).

Just as there is some evidence linking the Gnostics to the dissemination of the "authentic" portrait of Christ, so at the other end of the argument there is evidence—quite a lot of it— that Gnosticism flourished in Edessa until the fourth century.[22] Several of the Gnostic texts that were found at Nag Hammadi were translated into Coptic from Syriac originals. Specialists have suggested that one of these, the *Acts of Thomas*, was perhaps composed at Edessa in the second century. Another, *The First Apocalypse of James*, is tied to Edessa because of its references to Addai.[23] The most eminent man of letters that Edessa produced was heavily influenced by Gnosticism: Bardaisan (154–222) was both the most accomplished of Syriac poets and a philosophic teacher.[24] A century and a half after his death his teachings were assailed by St. Ephraim and other Edessan Christians, and he was reckoned by them as a Valentinian Gnostic. In fact, Bardaisan's writings indicate that he went beyond Gnosticism, combining it with Christianity and Stoicism. As late as 363 there were still Gnostics in Edessa, and when Arian Christians attacked them the emperor, Julian the Apostate, warned Edessa that he would not tolerate such municipal violence.[25] Taken together, considerable evidence testifies to Gnosticism at Edessa, and at an early date. In fact, some scholars have concluded that orthodox Christianity was relatively late in arriving at Edessa, and was preceded there not only by Gnosticism, but also by such other para-Christian groups as the Marcionites and the Bardaisanites. However that may be, I would suggest that in the first or second century, before Edessa had become "Christian" in any sense of the word, the Gnostics brought the Shroud to Edessa (as we have seen, "Hanan's portrait of Christ" was supposed to have come to Edessa before Addai converted the city to Christianity). Perhaps it stayed in Gnostic hands until the troubles of the fourth century: in Eusebius's time the Syriac story about Hanan's embassy apparently did not mention the portrait, but by the end of the fourth century a brief reference to the portrait was included in the *Doctrine of Addai.*

If, then, the Shroud should prove to be ancient, the circumstantial evidence would permit us to conclude that it was the Gnostics who preserved it until the third or fourth century, who painted portraits of Jesus in the tradition of the face imprinted on the Shroud (and who therefore were responsible for dissemination of the "authentic" portrait of Christ), and who brought the Shroud to Edessa. These conclusions about the Gnostics' custody of the Shroud, it is true, would require a radical revision of most scholars' opinions about the relationship of Gnosticism to Christianity, but the required revision would not be entirely novel. It is generally assumed that the non-orthodox followers of Christ "borrowed" Christ from orthodox Christianity. This assumption, Walter Bauer argued fifty years ago, rests on the suspect testimony of the Church Fathers.[26] The Fathers explained neatly and simply how the "true" understanding of Christ and his teachings had been preserved and broadcast, and how "erroneous" teachings about him had come about. Their explanation was as follows: (a) Before his passion, and in the forty days between his resurrection and his ascension into heaven, Jesus revealed all truth to his disciples. (b) After Christ's ascension, the disciples divided among themselves the responsibility for preaching the truth to all nations, and thus established the true church throughout the world. (c) Satan in his wicked envy beguiled the hearts of some Christians, who thereupon fell into error and general depravity and began promulgating false doctrines.

As the Church Fathers presented it, then, teachings about Christ that did not agree with the catholic position had never come to a country before the "truth," or independent of the truth, but were invariably a defection from the truth. Bauer's book made a very good case for a rather different sequence: (a) During the first and second centuries various religious groups who professed Christ—Gnostics, Jewish Christians, Marcionites, Ebionites, and others—flourished in parts of Asia Minor, in Egypt, and in eastern Syria (Edessa being an obvious illustration); at the same time, what would eventually become orthodoxy was taking root in those areas in which Paul had established churches, and especially in Rome itself. (b) In the third century "orthodoxy" expanded through the eastern provinces, at the expense of the "non-orthodox" groups of Christ-followers.[27]

Although the later Church Fathers believed that from the beginning there had been an unchanging, orthodox church to which the vast majority of Christ-followers had belonged, and that Christ-followers "outside the fold" were invariably defectors from within, the facts of the matter are demonstrably quite different. At the beginning of the second century there were several independent (and mutually hostile) factions of Christ-followers. On what might be called the right were very conservative Jewish followers of Christ, the Ebionites, who despised the Letters of Paul and who believed that Jesus not only obeyed the Torah scrupulously, but had in fact refined and sharpened it (although they regarded Jesus as entirely human—the son of Joseph—the Ebionites looked upon him as the True Prophet,

the Messiah of the Jewish people). In the center of the Christ-
followers at the beginning of the second century were those
whose creed would eventually be described as "orthodox": they
believed that Jesus, who was both human and divine, had for
the most part conformed to the Law of Moses even while
condemning the conventional piety, and that he had also—by
his death and resurrection—satisfied the Old Covenant once
and for all, and made compliance with the Law henceforth
unnecessary. On the left were Gnostics, who declared that Jesus
had condemned the Torah and the entire Jewish religious tradition
and had established a true religion, based on *gnosis.*

That each of these disparate groups of Christ-followers had
evolved during the first century is impossible to prove, since
the documents that have been preserved are those that were
approved by the triumphant orthodoxy. Even from Acts and
other canonical books of the New Testament, however, it is
evident that different trajectories were set very early. Before
Paul's conversion, and perhaps very soon after Jesus' crucifixion,
a radical group of Christ-followers was persecuted in Judaea
and dispersed: these first victims were the so-called Hellenists,
among whom Stephen the Martyr was a leader. These Hellenists,
it seems, were uncompromising and possibly somewhat hot-
headed, and it was apparently because of their outspoken
opposition to the Torah and the religious establishment (an
opposition in which they were said to have been encouraged
by their visions of the glorified Christ, standing at the right
hand of God) that they were lynched or banished. After their
departure and before the reign of Herod Agrippa (A.D. 41–44),
a more conservative group of Christ-followers became visible:
this was the group headed by Peter, James, and John. When
Herod Agrippa executed James and temporarily imprisoned Peter,
the leadership of this group passed to Jesus' brother, James the
Righteous. These "Hebrew" followers of Christ recommended
external compliance with the Torah, but celebrated Jesus as the
Messiah and as a worker of miracles. By the 50s Paul's congregations formed a third group, which in its attitude toward
the Torah was less radical than the Hellenists but less traditional
than the "Hebrews" who followed Peter and James. On the
matter of Jesus' nature and person, Paul had preached an

extraordinary doctrine: although Paul said nothing of Jesus as a miracle-worker, and emphasized the utter humiliation of both his life and death, he declared Jesus to be nothing less than an incarnation of God. Having left behind his mortal and crucified body—so Paul seems to have believed—Jesus ascended to heaven with a "spiritual" and immortal body.

Within this full spectrum of Christ-followers in the Apostolic Age, there is room for radicals who could have stood at the threshold of the Gnostic movement. They would presumably have been located near or among the so-called Hellenists. One of the seven Hellenist leaders mentioned in Acts 6 : 5 was a Nicolaus, whom later lore identified as the founder of the Nicolaitan sect. A more important figure, and apparently second only to Stephen in prominence, was the Philip whom historians customarily refer to as "Philip the Evangelist," to distinguish him from a more shadowy Philip listed among the Twelve. (The two Philips were sometimes regarded as the same person: for example, the author of the apocryphal *Acts of Philip* imagined his protagonist to have been both the apostle and the evangelist.) According to Acts 8 : 4–40, when Philip the Evangelist was expelled from Jerusalem he began to evangelize the Samaritans, and after much success in Samaria he carried his message to the coastal cities, from Azotus to Caesarea. The same tradition credited Philip with bringing the Gospel to two remarkable individuals: one an Ethiopian, in charge of Queen Candace's treasury, and the other the Samaritan Simon Magus (according to the author of Acts, Simon Magus was very quickly expelled from the movement by Peter). Thus, according to the traditions of orthodox Christians Simon was a Christ-follower at a time when Paul was still Saul, and a persecutor of Christ-followers. There is some reason to think that Simon's career may have peaked in A.D. 36. Josephus tells us that in that year there was a bloody upheaval in Samaria, when a multitude of apocalyptic Samaritans came to their holy mountain, Mt. Gerizim, and many were killed by Pontius Pilate's legionaries (because of his mis-handling of this affair, Pilate was dismissed as governor of Judaea and recalled to Rome). Since Acts 8 : 9–10 reports that the Samaritans "from the least to the greatest" followed Simon when he declared himself to be "some great one," it is possible that the Mt. Gerizim massacre in A.D. 36 involved Simon and his followers. As for Philip, by whom Simon had allegedly been baptized, at least his name was prestigious in Gnostic tradition: the Nag Hammadi texts included not only a *Gospel of Philip*, but also a *Letter of Peter to Philip*, and still another Gnostic text declares that Philip was the person who wrote down all of Jesus' deeds and speeches.

Although nothing here is at all certain, there is enough to suggest that at least some of the earliest Christ-followers were proto-Gnostics (this is what one would expect to find if the roots of Gnosticism do go back to the time of Philo and of John the Baptist). It is therefore no more likely that what we might call "Gnostic Christianity" was a deviation from what is traditionally called orthodox Christianity than that "orthodox" doctrines were deviations from a proto-Gnostic system. In *Gnosticism and Early Christianity* Grant emphasized how certain Gnostic influences are apparent in early writers—especially Paul and the author of the Gospel of John—whom in retrospect the orthodox Church would look back upon as perfectly orthodox.[28] Surely it is not too bold a suggestion that the Fourth Gospel and the Epistles of Paul represent not a veering of orthodoxy toward the temptations of Gnosticism, but rather a shift *away from* what we call "Gnostic" interpretations of Christ and toward what would eventually become the orthodox Christian interpretation. In the first century, undoubtedly, all followers of the *Christos* called themselves, and were called, *Christianoi.* But as the proportion of Gnostic Christ-followers declined within the overall "Christian" movement, their claim to be "Christian" at all may have become impossible to maintain in the face of orthodox opposition.

That the second-century Gnostics' traditions about Jesus were not a perversion of orthodoxy, but were rooted in Jesus' own teachings and crucifixion, is unequivocally denied by the Christian Church Fathers. Yet nothing less than that is implied if, as it seems, the Shroud was in the custody of Gnostic followers of Jesus before it passed into orthodox Christian hands. Let us take another, closer look at the evidence for this earliest chapter in the Shroud's history. Pieces of circumstantial evidence that support the thesis are the facts that there was a significant

Gnostic community in Edessa, and that the earliest known "authentic" portrait of Christ appears in a para-Christian tomb. A third circumstantial argument is that at least some of the Gnostics—the Carpocratians—had an attitude toward images very different from that of the Christians. Whereas the relatively conservative Christians inherited the Jewish antipathy to images, the more radical Gnostics showed an almost pagan enthusiasm for statues and painted portraits. These were not images of the Father, the High God of the Gnostics, but of the great teachers and philosophers, including the greatest of them all, Jesus. According to Irenaeus, the Carpocratians venerated these images in traditional pagan style, wreathing them with garlands and doing whatever else idolatry required.

An additional argument—more problematical, but also potentially more important—supports the contention that the Gnostics were the original custodians of the Shroud. This argument is furnished by a fragmentary text that its discoverer, Morton Smith, published in 1973.[29] It apparently comes from a "Secret Gospel of Mark," known to Clement of Alexandria at the end of the second century and quoted by Clement in a letter attacking the teachings of the Carpocratian Gnostics. According to Clement, this secret gospel told a story of Jesus' initiation of a young man, whom he had raised from the dead, into the mysteries of the Kingdom of God. For the initiation rite the young man was ordered to wrap his otherwise naked body in a *sindon*.[30] Smith's exhaustive commentary makes a convincing case that the story reflects a baptismal rite used by the Carpocratians and perhaps other Christ-followers in Alexandria. Although Smith proposed that this baptismal rite was practiced by Jesus himself, it is perhaps more credible that the rite was established by proto-Gnostic followers of Jesus in the decades following his crucifixion, and that it was established precisely because the proto-Gnostics had in their possession the original *sindon*—the Shroud, with its image of Jesus' naked body. For Clement's letter suggests that the Carpocratians' requirement that the initiate be naked within his *sindon* was somehow based on the nakedness of Jesus: the initiate is introduced "as naked man to naked man" (*gymnos gymnō*). We can only speculate about the meaning of this formula, but it may be that the Carpocratian baptismal ceremony involved some representation of Jesus' naked body, perhaps within a *sindon*.

Let us turn, then, to the most direct evidence that the Shroud was originally in the hands of the Gnostics: Irenaeus's specific testimony that the Carpocratian Gnostics had statues and portraits of Jesus that were supposedly based on a true image of Jesus, made "when he was among men." Irenaeus's mother-tongue was Greek, and he wrote in Greek. But the Greek text of his *Against Heresies* is lost, and we have only a Latin translation of that work. The portion of interest to us comes late in the first book; Irenaeus has already attacked the teachings and career of Simon Magus, of Basilides and other early Gnostics, and then takes up the Carpocratians (1.25.1): "They say that Jesus was begotten by Joseph, and that although he was like other humans, he was very different in respect to his soul. Because his soul was strong and pure, it had completely grasped everything that had appeared to it when it was in the realm of the unbegotten God." Irenaeus then berates the Carpocratians for their outrageous assertion that with true *gnosis* they could be on the same level with Peter and Paul, or even with Jesus himself. After pointing out more of their heretical views, Irenaeus continues as follows:

> *Gnosticos se autem vocant et imagines quasdam quidem depictas, quasdam autem et de reliqua materia fabricatas habent, dicentes formam Christi factam a Pilato illo tempore quo fuit Jesus cum hominibus; et has coronant et proponunt eas cum imaginibus mundi philosophorum, videlicet cum imagine Pythagorae et Platonis et Aristotelis et reliquorum et reliquam observationem circa eas similiter ut gentes faciunt.*[31]

(They call themselves Gnostics, and in fact they have images— some painted and some crafted out of one kind of material or another—claiming that a *forma* of Christ was made by Pilate at the time when Jesus was among men. These images they wreathe, and they place them among images of this world's philosophers, specifically of Pythagoras, Plato, Aristotle and the rest. As for the rest of the ritual observances of these images, they do just as the gentiles do.)

What Greek word did the Latin translator have in front of him when he wrote the words *formam Christi*? The Latin word *forma* may mean "form" or "impression," and has connotations of precise fidelity to the object from which it is made. Irenaeus's Greek word, which the Latin translator rendered as *formam*, was probably *ektypōma*. This is the word we find in a Greek paraphrase of Irenaeus's treatise, the *Against Heresies* of Epiphanius, the fourth-century bishop whom we met earlier in this chapter. Epiphanius paraphrased what he found in Irenaeus's book, and added one or two points of his own:

> That was the origin of those who are called Gnostics. They have images painted in colors, and some have images made of gold, silver or some other material. They say that there are some *ektypōmata* or other of Jesus, and that these *ektypōmata* were made by Pontius Pilate when Jesus dwelt with mankind. These images they keep hidden away. But they also have images of some philosophers—Pythagoras, Plato, Aristotle and others—and with these philosophers they have placed other images of Jesus; having set them up, they kneel before them and perform the rest of the gentile rituals.[32]

In yet another echo of Irenaeus's charge, Hippolytus, in the early third century, says that the Gnostics "make for themselves images of Christ, claiming that they [it?] came into being at that time through Pilate's agency." A somewhat different—but probably related—accusation attributed the possession of a Christ-image to the men who supposedly founded Gnosticism and its Carpocratian sect. According to this tradition, which survives only in a ninth-century treatise, Simon Magus and Carpocras "carried around with them an image of Christ."[33]

The phrase *ektypōma tou Christou* would have been appropriate for any exact replica of Jesus, whether a wax mould (like the Romans' *imagines*), or an imprint on cloth. As it happens, several Byzantine writers called the Edessan Icon, or the Mandylion, an *ektypōma*. Among others, the authors of the "Monthly Lection" and the "Festival Sermon" thus referred to the image of Christ on the cloth.[34] (They, of course, imagined that Christ himself had pressed the cloth to his face and had thus produced the *ektypōma*.)

At any rate, we learn from Irenaeus that in the second century the Carpocratian Gnostics venerated images of Jesus that were

said to have been based on a *forma Christi* that was not miraculous
and that was supposed to have been made by Pontius Pilate.
A curious parallel to this tradition, with the same ambiguity
between a singular image and plural images,[35] is found in a
Christian source of a later time. Antoninus of Placentia (Piacenza),
who made a pilgrimage through the East ca. 570, says that he
stopped and prayed in the courtroom, or Praetorium, where
Pilate heard the case against Jesus. In Pilate's Praetorium was
the stone slab on which Jesus, like all other defendants, had
been forced to stand (and Antoninus reports that the footprints
of Jesus were there to be seen in the slab, and that they show
Jesus' feet to have been beautiful, of average size, and graceful).
Also in Pilate's Praetorium there was a portrait of Jesus:

> *Statura communis, facies pulchra, capilli subanellati, manus for-*
> *monsae, digiti longi, quantum imago designat, quae illo vivente picta*
> *sunt, quae posita est in ipso praetorio.*[36]
>
> (His height was average, his face beautiful, his hair tended toward
> ringlets, his hands were very well formed, and his fingers were
> long, so far as the image shows, that were [sic] painted when he
> was alive, which is [sic] placed in the same Praetorium.)

We cannot be certain that the portrait Antoninus saw in Jerusalem
came from the same tradition as the Gnostics' portraits of Christ,
but in any case Antoninus's report shows that by the sixth
century some Christians *believed* what the Gnostics had believed
all along—that a tradition of Christ-portraits ultimately depended
on an image (in fact, a full-length image, showing the hands)
that was not miraculous and that had been made in Jesus' own
time.

In summary, one inference and one observation lead to a
tentative conclusion. First, if the Shroud is ancient, then—despite
the opinions of the Church Fathers—the long-haired, bearded
representation of Jesus that appears in Roman art of the third
and fourth century was intended as an authentic portrait, the
Shroud being the archetype of this portrait tradition. Second,
the Gnostics at a very early period venerated images of Jesus
that were believed to be authentic portraits and that were said
to depend on a *forma Christi* made by Pilate. Our conditional
conclusion is inescapable: if the Shroud does bear, as it seems

to, the direct image of Jesus' body, then the *forma Christi* preserved by the Gnostics was the Shroud.

When was this original *forma* said to have been made? The Christian Antoninus supposed that a portrait was painted "when Jesus was alive," but the Gnostics' tradition about their *forma Christi* is not clear. They may have explained that Pilate ordered it made while Jesus was being tried, scourged, and mocked with a crown of thorns. But there is a more obvious possibility. Because the Gnostics did not believe in the bodily resurrection of Jesus, it is possible that they said that Pilate ordered the *forma Christi* made after the crucifixion, from the dead body of Christ.

vii / The Sindon

WE have finally come to the beginning of the Shroud's history. The question that must finally be answered is: What is the Shroud, and how could the image of Jesus' body have been imprinted upon it? The alternative explanations can be sharply drawn. For those who believe that the Shroud carries the true image of Jesus, the answer for the last six centuries has usually been that the Shroud is in fact a burial shroud, and that it was miraculously imprinted in the tomb, perhaps when Jesus' dead body was brought back to life. The alternative is that the Shroud is not a shroud, but an imprinter's canvas, and that from Jesus' body the imprinters made the image visible on the Shroud. Although it would be gratifying to find that the image is miraculous, the historical evidence points unequivocally to the second alternative: the imprint on the Shroud is the work of human hands.

That the Shroud is not in fact a burial shroud is suggested, first of all, by the fact that it bears no resemblance to any shroud known from antiquity. It was the custom in Hellenistic and Roman times, as it is today, to dress the dead in fine clothes, the kind of clothes worn by the living on special occasions. A Roman was carried to the funeral pyre in his toga, and a Greek was buried in a fine tunic and himation. The Greeks might also place the corpse in an open box or coffin and then drape it with a sheet or cover, so that the corpse in its coffin resembled a person asleep in a bed. In no case was the cover pulled over the face of the corpse, as was the Shroud. Such coverings were apparently about one-third the length of the Shroud. Altogether, the funerary clothes and coverings were referred to as *entaphia*.[1]

During most of antiquity the Jews, like the Greeks and Romans, clothed their dead as they had been clothed in life. When, in the second century B.C., belief in a resurrection began, it was widely believed that the dead would be raised in the same clothes in which they had been buried. During the first century it is possible, as the Gospel of John indicates, that many Jews adopted the practice of anointing a corpse with spices and then wrapping it, like a mummy, in linen strips. These are the only alternatives. Burial of a naked corpse in a linen sheet is unexampled in Jewish literary sources.[2] In Egypt, the entire body—either wrapped as a mummy or, in Christian times, clothed in a cap, tunic, and sandals—was covered with a linen cloth. These Egyptian shrouds, many of which were discovered in a cemetery at Panopolis, were regularly about 8 feet long and 4 feet wide.[3] Almost all the ancient textiles known today were found in tombs, and it is remarkable that none of these funerary cloths begins to approximate the dimensions of the Shroud.

Those dimensions at first glance seem impractical: the cloth is just over 14 feet long, it is 3 feet 7 inches wide, and before the additional strip was sewn along the left side its width was only 3 feet 3½ inches. A linen cloth of that size would have been too long and too narrow to serve as a doubled sheet in which to sleep, nor is there any other routine activity for which the cloth could conceivably have been used. Thus we have a cloth with no obvious utility, and with dimensions that have no parallel from the ancient world. And for what we find on this cloth—the frontal and dorsal images of a man—there is also no parallel. Is it a coincidence that for the portrayal of these images the cloth's otherwise inexplicable dimensions are indispensable? The reasonable inference would be that the cloth was woven to its extraordinary dimensions *in order* to serve the single purpose that it has served: the portrayal of an imprint of a man's body.

It is also pertinent, as most sindonologists have observed, that this particular cloth was not draped over Jesus' body as a covering sheet would have been, but instead was tautly suspended over the body. In the words of Ian Wilson, who favors the miraculous explanation of the image, "a first, essential condition for what is visible on the Shroud has to be that the position of the cloth was relatively flat over the body." For in no other way could a three-dimensional or "global" image have been transferred to the cloth. (If the imprint had been made with the cloth draped over the torso, for example, when the cloth was removed from the body and laid flat a torso-image would have appeared whose width was the equivalent of the front and the two sides of the torso.) That the cloth was just as flat on the frontal side of the body as on the dorsal side was dramatically confirmed by John Jackson and his associates, who tested a photograph of the Shroud with an "image analyzer" that had originally been developed to analyze photographs sent back to earth from space. The VP-8 Image Analyzer showed that the image on the Shroud was "three-dimensional in that information defining the spatial contours of Jesus' body are encoded in the varying intensity levels of the image." The implication, according to Jackson, is that "the lay of the Shroud was relatively flat."[4] Why and how a burial shroud would have been suspended like a flat roof over the body, with the unwashed body lying naked beneath it, cannot be reasonably explained. Ian Wilson suggests that "this may well have been made possible by the packing of blocks of aromatic spices around the body in the tomb,"[5] but in proposing that awkward reconstruction Wilson must accept the statement at John 19 : 39 that Joseph of Arimathea and Nicodemus brought a great quantity of spices to the tomb, and must reject the very next verse's statement that Joseph and Nicodemus then wrapped the body, with the spices, in strips of linen cloth.

The image of the head on the Shroud provides additional evidence that the cloth was artificially suspended: there are two parallel strips at the sides of the face, on which the image was faintly transferred. As a pamphlet published by the Holy Shroud Guild has stated, "from the imprint it is clear that at either side of the head there was some kind of support which held the cloth practically flat."[6] Again, no persuasive argument can be made why Joseph should have taken such elaborate precautions to keep the cloth flat and taut, while neglecting the obvious and essential obligation of washing and clothing the body. On the other hand, some framework of slats or laths might have been necessary for keeping the cloth taut during an imprinting.

And for whatever purpose an imprint of Jesus' crucified body may have been made, that purpose would have been frustrated by clothing or even washing the body. Thus the features of the Shroud's image that are most troublesome to an interpretation of the Shroud as a burial shroud are readily explicable if one interprets the Shroud as an imprinter's canvas.

Although important, these technical arguments are finally insufficient, because they underscore how many technical questions remain. Scientists believe that the image is the result of fibril degradation, but there is no satisfactory explanation of how the image was produced. This ignorance, of course, has more than anything else encouraged the belief that the image is miraculous: if we cannot duplicate it, only a miracle could have produced it. Such reasoning has always had popular appeal. Many classical Greeks, admiring the colossal boulders their Bronze Age ancestors had used in building the citadel-wall at Mycenae, spoke of the masonry as "Cyclopean": mere humans, it was said, could not have moved such enormous stones, and therefore the giants whom Homer called Cyclopes must have built Mycenae's walls. In our own time, millions of readers have been intrigued by Erich Von Daniken's speculation that many "inexplicable" achievements of the distant past—from the Nazca lines in Peru to the pyramids of Egypt—must have been accomplished with the help of superhuman extraterrestrials, who journeyed to and departed from our planet in "chariots of the gods."

Historians do not generally subscribe to such theories, but are instead persuaded that past (like present) phenomena have a natural explanation, even though in some instances that explanation has not yet been found. Several of the technologies of the past have been unusually difficult to identify. The ingenious ancient art of granulation, familiar to goldsmiths in the Near Eastern and Classical worlds, was forgotten during medieval times. As Etruscan and Greek jewelry came to light in the nineteenth century, attempts were made to copy the exquisite ancient work, but the modern products were clumsy and unattractive. Finally, in March 1933, H. A. P. Littledale hit upon and patented the ancient technique. Another mystery was the lustrous black glaze that is so distinctive of Athenian vase painting. Repeated efforts to duplicate the glaze were unsuccessful until Dr. Theodor Schumann discovered its secret in 1942. Equally frustrating has been the attempt to discover how the Stradivari and the Guarneri families manufactured their incomparable violins in Cremona in the seventeenth and early eighteenth centuries. Thus is the historian occasionally humbled by the recognition that—despite our own generation's arrogant assumption that modern technology enables us to accomplish anything accomplished in the past—our ancestors did from time to time use their primitive technology to create things that cannot now be either duplicated or fully explained.

When in the sixth century the Edessans began to venerate the cloth that, it seemed, had saved their city from Chosroes, they proclaimed it *acheiropoietos*—not made by human hands. Although they tried on occasion to copy it, they obviously did not know the technique of producing such an image. Like the sixth-century Edessans, many modern sindonologists regard the Shroud as *acheiropoietos*, for no reason other than their inability to duplicate its image. In the earlier Roman East, however, the technique for producing such an image as the Shroud's must have been available. Although extraordinary, it must have been employed often enough that several of its products survived antiquity. For the Shroud's image seems not to have been unique. When the Edessans proclaimed that their icon was not made by human hands, several other cities in eastern Asia Minor could boast a cloth that also bore an *acheiropoietos* image. In Cappadocia three cities—Melitene (Malatya), Camulia, and Caesarea—exhibited linen cloths, each of which bore an image claimed as *acheiropoietos* (the Camulian cloth was taken to Constantinople in 574).[7] A similar cloth was in Diobulion, a Pontic town near the city of Amaseia (present-day Amasya).[8] All of these were, in the late sixth century, explained as images of Christ, and as miraculously created or copied. And in the Egyptian city of Memphis a linen with a barely perceptible image of a child was explained, again in the late sixth century, as effected by Jesus when he came to Egypt as an infant.[9] None of these other cloths is extant, and we cannot prove, even though we must suspect, that the images that they bore had been made in the same way that the Shroud's image was made. What we seem to be dealing with here is an imprinting procedure, perhaps some kind of thermography, that was forgotten before the end of antiquity, and whose few surviving products were, in the sixth century, interpreted as supernaturally created.[10]

The most telling evidence that the Shroud's image was not the miraculous result of Jesus' resurrection is the Carpocratian Gnostics' tradition that an *ektypōma* of Christ was made by Pontius Pilate, and their belief that Jesus' body was not resurrected from the tomb. The Gnostics firmly believed in an afterlife, but an afterlife in which the disembodied soul lived in the Fullness of the Father. And when the Gnostics spoke of the resurrection of Jesus, which they regularly did, "resurrection" meant the soul's return from its bodily prison. In his appearances after his death, they said, Jesus was seen as a luminous being, a dazzling light. What happened to Jesus' body the Gnostic literature thus far discovered does not explicitly state, but seems to assume that, like all other bodies, it returned to the dust. If the Gnostics' *forma Christi* was the Shroud—and there is no real alternative if the Shroud does indeed carry the direct imprint of Jesus' body—then the Shroud was not regarded by its earliest custodians as a document of a miracle that had happened to Jesus' body. At the risk of being repetitious, I will put the argument the other way round: the Carpocratian Gnostics' tradition that their *forma Christi* was man-made makes it very difficult to believe that our Shroud was miraculously imprinted; for if our Shroud does in fact carry the true image of Jesus' body, the only object with which our Shroud can be identified in the first and second centuries is the Gnostics' *forma Christi*. In the fourth century the Edessan Christians also seem to have regarded the same image as man-made (they, however, described it as a painting, painted by Hanan), and their opinion is also of value. But far more reliance can be placed on what the Gnostics had to say about it in the second century. For the Gnostics of Irenaeus's day would not only have been chronologically much closer to the Shroud's origins, but they also seem to have known what sort of image it was: they described it not as a painting, but as an *ektypōma*. Whether or not the second-century Gnostics were familiar with the technique that produced the imprint, the crucial point is that they understood the imprint to have been wrought by human hands.

If one concedes that the *forma Christi* of the Gnostics was the Shroud, and therefore that the Gnostics considered the Shroud's image to be man-made, could one still go on to argue that the Gnostics were trying to conceal a miracle, and that the Shroud's image had in fact been miraculously produced in the tomb? Had there been any belief, in the first or second century, that the Shroud's image was miraculous, surely orthodox Christians would have voiced it. The orthodox Christians, who devoted their lives to convincing the world that Jesus had risen bodily from the tomb, could not possibly have kept silent about an image that they thought had been miraculously imprinted on his burial shroud when his body was in the tomb. Some have tried to reconcile that silence with the miraculous interpretation of the Shroud, arguing that although the first Christians considered the Shroud miraculous, they chose not to mention it, either because the Shroud showed Jesus naked or because it had been in contact with a corpse and was therefore unclean. In other words, because of their modesty or their devotion to ritual law, the first Christians did not mention the visible and demonstrable miracle that God had placed in their hands on Easter morning. This is not a reasonable argument.

To the contrary, it appears that orthodox Christians knew about the Shroud, and tried to minimize it. In the late second century, we have seen, Irenaeus attacked the Gnostics' claims about their *forma Christi*, and the orthodox writers who echoed his charges certainly implied that the Gnostics' *ektypōma* was either fraudulent or of minor significance. There are also hints that long before Irenaeus's time orthodox Christians were concerned about the cloth. If the Gnostics treasured the Shroud in the first century, undoubtedly other Christ-followers of the time would also have known of its existence and of its portrayal of Jesus' crucified body. It may have been to offset the Gnostics' explanation of the *forma Christi* that the orthodox told the story that Joseph of Arimathaea, before placing Jesus' body in the tomb, wrapped it in a linen sheet, a *sindon*, that he had purchased. This story, common to all the Synoptic Gospels, ostensibly serves no purpose in the narrative of Jesus' passion and resurrection.

But to the first-century Christian who was worried by the report that the Gnostics' cloth was imprinted by Pilate after the crucifixion, the story of Joseph's *sindon* would have given comfort and assurance. For with that story the orthodox could suppose that the Gnostics' cloth was not an imprinter's canvas, and that whatever image was on the cloth was merely the "natural" impression that a dead body might over two days leave on a linen sheet. The Gospel of John does not mention the sheet and instead says that Joseph and Nicodemus, after wrapping the limbs, with spices, in linen strips, placed a "sweat-cloth" (*soudarion*) over Jesus' face.[11] Since the Gospel of John was written several decades later than the Synoptic Gospels, perhaps its author had heard of the *ektypōma* only in its frame, displaying no more than Jesus' face.

If one looks at the period before "orthodox" Christians were clearly differentiated from other groups of Christ-followers, and before the Synoptic Gospels had been written, one can possibly find dim reflections of an imprinted *sindon* in the letters of Paul. The dimmest of these might be Paul's persistent equation of the Christian community with "the body of Christ." More pointedly, in his references to baptism (a good example is Galatians 3 : 27–28) Paul describes the initiate as clothing himself in Christ, as in a garment. In a metaphorical sense "to put on Christ" of course meant to enter the Christian community, and the phrase has traditionally been understood as never having been more than a metaphor. But it is not inconceivable that the phrase once had a literal meaning: part of a baptismal ritual reported to Paul may have been the "putting on" of an image of Jesus. These possible reflections, however, can at best suggest a second-hand knowledge of the Shroud. Quite obviously, an imprinted *sindon* could have played no part in Paul's own ministry.

Early in the second century, by which time "orthodox" and Gnostic Christians were bitter antagonists, the orthodox seem to have had an explanation for the fact that their community was not in possession of the *sindon*. Although the New Testament Gospels describe the *sindon* as a linen sheet in which Joseph wrapped the body of Jesus before burial, they do not explain what happened to the *sindon* after Jesus arose and left the tomb. Another fairly early text, however, gives us the story. The second-

century *Gospel according to the Hebrews*, composed originally in
Hebrew or Aramaic, was translated into both Greek and Latin
by St. Jerome. Neither the original nor the translations have
survived. But in the course of an essay on Jesus' brother, James
the Righteous, Jerome had occasion to quote the following passage
from his Latin translation of the *Gospel according to the Hebrews:*

> *Dominus autem cum dedisset sindonem servo Sacerdotis, ivit ad
> Jacobum, et apparuit ei. Juraverat enim Jacobus, se non comesturum
> panem ab illa hora qua biberat calicem Domini, donec viderat eum
> resurgentem a dormientibus.*[12]

> (And when the Lord had given the *sindon* to the high priest's
> slave, he went to James, and appeared to him. For James had
> sworn that he would not eat bread from the time that he drank
> the Lord's cup until he saw the Lord risen from those who sleep.)

Jerome quotes the old gospel to illustrate the firmness of James's
faith that Jesus would arise from the dead. For our purposes,
however, what is of interest is the reference to the linen sheet,
the *sindon* (even in this Latin text, the Greek word is retained):
after his resurrection, Jesus gave the *sindon* to the high priest's
slave. That detail implies not only that the *sindon* was in existence
when the gospel was composed, but also that it was not in
orthodox hands. If the Gnostics were the Shroud's first custodians,
as they seem to have been, orthodox Christians would necessarily
have had some explanation of how this cloth, which the orthodox
were then describing as a *sindon* in which Joseph had wrapped
the body of Jesus before placing it in the tomb, happened to
fall into the hands of the Satanic Gnostics. The fragment from
the *Gospel according to the Hebrews* may show a part of that
explanation (the complementary story would have had to tell
how Simon Magus acquired the *sindon* from the high priest).[13]

A more direct denial of Pilate's *forma Christi* was the Edessan
Christians' attempt to explain it away. Perhaps even when it
was in Gnostic hands, and certainly after they had taken it over,
the Christian authorities said that it was a painting rather than
an imprint, and that it had been made before Jesus' passion by
Hanan, a skilled painted and the courier of King Abgar. Most
audacious was their pretense that only the face of Jesus was
portrayed on the cloth. People have always had an extraordinary

capacity to believe what they wish to believe, and it may be that even in the fourth century the Christian hierarchy in Edessa was able to convince itself that the cloth in fact was a portrait presented to King Abgar. As time went on, the weight of tradition and the pressure of conformity would have prevented anyone from doubting the received explanation. The image of Jesus' naked and apparently bloodied body was not readily compatible with the story, but the custodians successfully dealt with the matter by preventing access to the cloth, and by permitting no mention of the full image. The story of "Hanan's portrait of Christ" may have helped to extinguish the Gnostics' explanation of their *forma Christi*. But it is today decisive evidence that orthodox Christians saw the cloth as an obstacle, and not as proof of their belief that Jesus' body had arisen from the grave.

*   *   *

If, as the limited evidence indicates, the Shroud was in the hands of the Gnostics before it passed to the orthodox, the Gnostics' explanation of the image deserves critical attention. They attributed the original *forma Christi* to Pontius Pilate. The main point is that they regarded the *forma Christi* as a human artifact, rather than as a miracle. But it is also of some importance whether their attribution of the image to Pilate was right or wrong, even though there is no way of proving or disproving the Gnostics' claim. The notion that Pilate had an imprint made from Jesus' body seems far-fetched, although it is not impossible. On the other hand, it is obviously also possible that the imprint may have been made by some of Jesus' own following, by followers who would become the founders of Christian Gnosticism. In that case, there would be no need to wonder how the Gnostics could have acquired a *forma Christi* that had been made by Pilate. That these followers of Jesus would have claimed that Pilate was responsible for an imprint that they themselves had made is surely a reasonable possibility in a society that opposed—sometimes violently—the making of images, that abhorred the display of the naked body, and that had strict regulations concerning the burial of a corpse. One cannot imagine why the Roman governor would have wanted to make an imprint of Jesus' body, and perhaps it is less difficult to suppose that some persons whom Jesus had attracted might have done so. Among the Greeks living in the Egyptian Fayyum, a bereaved family customarily hired an artist to make an encaustic painting of the deceased, and the portrait—often strikingly realistic— was then attached to the deceased's coffin. When a Roman magistrate died, a wax mask of his features was made imme- diately, and in the houses of the nobility these wax masks— *imagines*—of prominent ancestors were kept in the atrium. In the case of the Shroud, the image was of the entire body. Perhaps those who made it wished not only to preserve a likeness of Jesus' face, but also to have a permanent record of his violent death. That Pilate should have wished to have a document of the crucifixion is less likely than that some of Jesus' followers were determined that his death should never be forgotten. This determination resounds in the words of the ritual that was already established before the conversion of Paul: "Take eat, this is my body . . . , take drink, this is my blood . . . , this do in remembrance of me."

Might it have been the Hellenist Christ-followers, those im- pulsive nonconformists among whom Stephen and Philip were counted, who saw to the Shroud's imprinting? That possibility has some support in the ancient testimony. The Gospel of Matthew (28 : 11–15) shows that in the latter half of the first century there was a "widely known" story that Jesus' disciples surreptitiously disposed of his body. A more obvious possibility is that Joseph of Arimathaea arranged for the imprinting of the *sindon.* In the New Testament, Joseph is the devout purchaser of the *sindon,* and the burier of Jesus' body. But the second- century Gospel of Peter suggests that Joseph, a "friend of Pilate," once played a more complex role in the accounts of Jesus' death and burial.

Wherever and by whomever the imprint was made, it is not likely to have been made by those men and women who first declared and believed that Jesus had arisen bodily from the tomb. Since "orthodox" Christians were not in possession of the cloth from the time of the Synoptic Gospels' composition through at least the late second century, there is little reason to suppose that the group's earliest representatives had had custody of it. In addition, the hostility with which Irenaeus regarded the Gnostics' claim about their *forma Christi* is fairly clear evidence that the image had from the outset been alien to orthodox traditions.

The important implication of this history of the Shroud is that the proto-Gnostic Christ-followers knew more than did the proto-orthodox about the aftermath of Jesus' crucifixion. For whether the imprint was made by Pilate or by the Gnostics' spiritual forebears, in the second century the Gnostics seem to have had the cloth, and to have known something about its imprinting. Thus the Gnostics' denial of Jesus' bodily resurrection from the tomb would not have originated as anti-Christian polemic, but would be a lingering echo of the account that had been passed down to them by those persons who had attended to Jesus' body. The proto-Gnostics' traditions about what happened after Jesus' crucifixion would very likely not have been limited to the negative statement that Jesus' body did not come back to life. What *did* happen may also have been declared, although not publicly. The proto-Gnostics may have reported that after the imprint was made the body was buried, although in that case a story probably would have transpired about the final resting-place of Jesus' body. It is also possible that they reported something outrageous, which therefore had to be kept secret: for example, that in defiance of traditional Jewish practice, the body, like that of a sacrificial lamb, was burned. But whatever reports the proto-Gnostics may have had about the imprinting and its aftermath are lost, and we have only the Gnostic traditions that Jesus' immortal soul appeared to his followers after his death.

The proto-Gnostics' view of Jesus' physical death and spiritual "resurrection" may at the outset have been denounced only by Pharisees, Sadducees, and others who had opposed Jesus. But as the years passed, perhaps the proto-Gnostic view also came under attack from the opposite direction, as the belief took root—nurtured, undoubtedly, by Paul's ambiguous statements on the subject—that Jesus had come back to life physically. This belief spread rapidly, and as it spread the proto-Gnostics' belief in Jesus' spiritual "resurrection" may have become conspicuous, and have been seen by the proto-orthodox as a treacherous compromise. For although the proto-Gnostics may initially have regarded the fate of Jesus' body as a matter of minor importance, the burgeoning orthodox church was founded squarely on the belief in Jesus' bodily resurrection. In the second and third centuries the Gnostics' denial of that resurrection seemed to be an heretical deviation from orthodox teaching. But the Shroud implies that the Gnostics' understanding was the earlier of the two.

The Shroud, therefore, seems to support what New Testament scholars have been saying all along: belief in the resurrection of Jesus' earthly body did not begin until some decades after the crucifixion. As James M. Robinson recently summarized in his presidential address to the Society of Biblical Literature,[14] it was between the time of Paul and the end of the first century that Christians began defining the resurrection of Jesus as the return to life of his nail-pierced, buried body. Until the time of Paul, followers of the crucified Jesus had declared only that after his death Jesus from time to time, in a luminous or spiritual form, had appeared to them, and so had proved his triumph over death. By the end of the first century, the Gnostic insistence that Jesus' soul was immortal had crystallized, and also the opposing orthodox belief that Jesus had come back to life bodily, walking, talking, eating, and drinking with his disciples. As phrased by another New Testament scholar, "the dominant image of Jesus' resurrection" in the first decades after the crucifixion "seems to have been not the resuscitation of his corpse, as it is depicted in the passion narratives of the canonical gospels and Acts, but his exaltation and enthronement in heaven."[15]

And so, by a supreme irony, the Shroud may indeed provide mute but critical testimony on the doctrine of Jesus' physical resurrection. If it is indeed ancient, as it seems to be, the Shroud dissolves the credibility of the doctrine. And it implies that Jesus himself declared—as his Gnostic followers continued to declare—that we are a divine spirit in mortal shells.

*   *   *

If this is the story of the Shroud, it is a story of paradox and accidents so astounding that it seems to have been written by a mischievous providence. The imprint that the Gnostics cherished as "Pilate's *forma Christi*" was taken over by the

[handwritten: Jesus' disciple ↑ one of 70 Thaddeus gave it to Edessa]

[handwritten: wrong]

Christians of Edessa, and so survived when everything else associated with Gnosticism was ferreted out and destroyed by orthodox Christians. And while most cities of the Roman Empire, including Rome itself, were being plundered, "Hanan's portrait of Christ" remained safe in Edessa, the blessed city whose good fortune convinced contemporaries that the Letter of Jesus guaranteed the city's security. Finally, Edessa's turn came in 544, as the Letter's protective power seemed to fail. But at the very last moment, and contrary to all expectations, the city was saved from Chosroes, and the instrument of its salvation seemed to be nothing other than the portrait. Exalted to supernatural status, the Edessan Icon weathered the century of Iconoclasm, during which most representational art of the Orthodox world disappeared. In 944, the Mandylion was removed to Constantinople, and so was no longer in Edessa when that city's Christian heritage was destroyed. Constantinople, too, eventually fell to the Turks, but by that time the Mandylion had been stolen and taken to France. Emerging there as the Holy Shroud, it survived two successive bishops' efforts to do away with it. Then on 4 December 1532 the Shroud came within minutes of destruction, when fire broke out in the Sainte Chapelle in Chambéry where the Shroud was kept. The Shroud itself caught fire, but the fire was extinguished, having done no damage to the image, but leaving scorch marks which in 1973 and 1978 proved useful to scientists analyzing the image. From France the Shroud was taken to Turin, consequently avoiding the French Revolution, in which many less fortunate Christian relics perished. Thus the Shroud survived into the age of science. Although other sacred relics withered in that harsh climate, the Shroud did not. Photography revealed something in the Shroud that nobody had suspected, and that the ancient imprinters had not intended. And so, of the billions of people who lived before the invention of photography, there is a photographic likeness of only one— Jesus Christ. Finally, the sole relic from the event that created an entire civilization, a relic which for almost a millenium Christians zealously preserved as Jesus' gift to Abgar, a relic which for the last six hundred years has seemed to be a document of Jesus' resurrection, turns into evidence that Jesus and his

[handwritten left margin: Providence]

[handwritten left margin: a lie →]

[handwritten bottom: Imprint is definately caused by Jesus' Bodily Resurrection. Is. 26:19 Is. 53:11]

earliest followers believed not in the resurrection of the body but in the immortality of the soul. *A Blatant LIE*

Such will be the story of the Shroud, if testing proves the Shroud to be an ancient cloth. The story will include no miracles. It will ~~not need~~ them.
demand

This author has no way of showing how image arrived on cloth other than bodily Resurrection of Jesus!

Notes

Chapter I: Historians and the Shroud

1. Pietro Savio, *Ricerche storiche sulla Santa Sindone* (Turin: Società editrice internazionale, 1957); Ian Wilson, *The Shroud of Turin*, rev. ed. (New York: Image Books, 1979). The first edition of Wilson's book appeared in 1978.

2. Although now somewhat outdated, the best bibliography on the Shroud—containing almost 300 entries—is in a frankly confessional book, Edward A. Wuenschel's *Self-Portrait of Christ: The Holy Shroud of Turin* (Esopus, N.Y.: Holy Shroud Guild, 1957), pp. 103–21.

3. For the lives and accomplishments of prominent first-generation sindonologists, see John Walsh, *The Shroud* (New York: Random House, 1963).

4. Ernst von Dobschuetz, *Christusbilder. Untersuchungen zur christlichen Legende* (Leipzig: J. C. Hinrichs'sche Buchhandlung, 1899), p. 76, n. 3.

5. Although his first book on the subject appeared in 1899, the most important of Chevalier's six books on the Shroud was *Etude critique sur l'origine du Saint Suaire de Lirey-Chambéry-Turin* (Paris: A. Picard, 1900). Chevalier's sixth and last book on the Shroud was published in 1903.

6. Wuenschel, *Self-Portrait of Christ*, pp. 18 and 28.

7. Herbert Thurston, "The Holy Shroud and the Verdict of History," and "The Holy Shroud as a Scientific Problem," *The Month* 101 (1903): 17–29, 162–78.

8. For a further description of this remarkable work of scholarship, see Chapter IV, note 2.

9. Paul Vignon, *Le Saint Suaire de Turin devant la science, l'archéologie, l'histoire, l'iconographie, la logique* (Paris: Masson, 1939).

10. Pierre Barbet's work was translated from the French and published in this country as *Doctor at Calvary* (New York: P. J. Kenedy and Sons, 1953; reprint New York, Image Books, 1963).

11. For a critical appraisal of the Turin hierarchy's attitude toward research on the Shroud, see Peter Rinaldi's "Turin and the Holy Shroud," in *Proceedings of the 1977 United States Conference of Research on the Shroud of Turin* (New York: Holy Shroud Guild, 1977), pp. 10–12.

12. For the report of the 1969 commission, see Chapter II, note 1.

13. Wilson gave a preview of his conclusions in "The Shroud's History Before the 14th Century," in *Proceedings 1977*, pp. 31–49.

14. Although a full report of the 1978 tests has not yet been published, much of the essential material had been set out by L. A. Schwalbe and R. N.

Rogers in "Physics and Chemistry of the Shroud of Turin: A Summary of the 1978 Investigation," *Analytica Chimica Acta* 135 (1982): 3–49.

Chapter II: A Description of the Shroud and Its Image

1. Professor Raes' report was initially published in *La S. Sindone: Ricerche e studi della commissione di esperti nominata dall' Archivescovo di Torino, Card. Michele Pellegrino, nel 1969* (special issue of the *Rivista diocesana torinese*, Turin, 1976). The 1969 commission's report has been translated into English and is available as *Report of the Turin Commission on the Holy Shroud* (London: Screenpro Films [5 Meard St., London W1V 3HQ], 1976). For Professor Raes' findings, see pp. 79–83 of that publication. For a thorough summary and discussion, see Wilson, *Shroud*, pp. 68–72.

2. For a careful, comprehensive, and up-to-date study, see John Tyrer, "Looking at the Turin Shroud as a Textile," *Shroud Spectrum International* 2 (1983): 35–45. Unfortunately, no good book exists on ancient textiles, nor any study that inventories all the textiles from antiquity that have been found. R. J. Forbes devoted all of vol. 4 of his massive antiquarian series, *Studies in Ancient Technology* (Leiden: Brill, 1964), to textiles, but took little note of archaeological evidence.

3. M. Popham, E. Touloupa, and H. Sackett, "The Hero of Lefkandi," *Antiquity* 56 (1982): 169–74.

4. On the linens in the tomb of Thutmose IV, see Elizabeth Riefstahl, *Thebes in the Time of Amunhotep III* (Norman: University of Oklahoma Press, 1964), p. 49. For the Tutankhamen textiles, see Howard Carter and A. C. Mace, *The Tomb of Tutankhamen* (New York: Cooper Square, 1963), Vol. 2, pp. 185–86; Vol. 3, pp. 124–26.

5. Frei's full list of pollens is given by Wilson as Appendix E, *Shroud*, pp. 293–98. On the 1978 findings, cf. Schwalbe and Rogers, "Physics," pp. 46–47, n. 4: "Very few pollen were observed on the tape samples taken in the present Project, and no effort was made to identify them." For the American team's reaction to Frei's procedures, see the amusing account in John H. Heller's *Report on the Shroud of Turin* (New York: Houghton Mifflin, 1983), p. 108.

6. Cf. Wilson, *Shroud*, p. 250: "Other shrouds have survived . . . A few, including those of known martyrs, bear imprints—but nothing approaching the perfect photographic likeness of the Shroud of Turin." I have seen no specific or documented reference to any of these shrouds. Before the nineteenth century, apparently, there were a great many cloths said to be ancient and which did bear human images, but the assumption today is that these were painted images. According to Thomas Humber, *The Sacred Shroud* (New York: Pocket Books, 1977), p. 78, "in medieval Europe there were at least forty-three 'True Shrouds,' both plain and figured." Von Dobschuetz's catalogue of "True Shrouds," however, included among the figured examples only the Shroud of Turin, the Besançon Shroud, and a cloth (which did not survive the Middle Ages) in Lisbon. See *Christusbilder*, p. 73, n. 3.

7. Robert Wilcox, *Shroud* (New York: Macmillan, 1977), pp. 60–67, including Wilcox's full-page photograph, on p. 61, of one of the stained tunics.

8. Ibid., pp. 30–34.

9. Schwalbe and Rogers, "Physics," pp. 36–40. Chapter 7 ("Is There Actual Blood on the Shroud?") of Ian Wilson's *Shroud* is now outdated, because this excellent book went to press before the results of the 1978 tests were available.

10. Schwalbe and Rogers, "Physics" (see bibliography).

11. See note 1, this chapter.

12. Schwalbe and Rogers, "Physics," p. 14.

13. For a sympathetic summary of McCrone's several publications, see Joe Nickell, *Inquest on the Shroud of Turin* (Buffalo, N.Y.: Prometheus Books, 1983), pp. 119–25.

14. J. H. Heller and A. D. Adler, "A Chemical Investigation of the Shroud of Turin," *Canadian Society of Forensic Science Journal* 14 (1981): 81–103. For a popular account of his dispute with McCrone, see Heller, *Report*, pp. 135 ff.

15. Nickell, *Inquest*, p. 133 (Nickell is here quoting his collaborator, physicist Marvin M. Mueller).

16. Schwalbe and Rogers, "Physics," pp. 24 ff.; cf. Nickell, *Inquest*, pp. 135–36.

17. Kenneth E. Stevenson and Gary R. Habermas, *Verdict on the Shroud* (Wayne, Penna.: Dell/Banbury, 1981), p. 91 and passim; for other formulations of this same thesis see Geoffrey Ashe, "What Sort of Picture," *Sindon* 1966, p. 18. (*Sindon* is published by the Centro Internazionale di Sindonologia, in Turin); Wilcox, *Shroud*, pp. 171–73; Wilson, *Shroud*, p. 250.

18. Schwalbe and Rogers, "Physics," p. 27.

19. Stevenson and Habermas, *Verdict on the Shroud*, p. 117; cf. Schwalbe and Rogers, "Physics," pp. 25–26.

20. Ashe, "What Sort of Picture," pp. 15–19.

21. Schwalbe and Rogers, "Physics," p. 28.

22. Ibid., p. 27.

23. S. F. Pellicori and M. S. Evans, "The Shroud of Turin Through the Microscope," *Archaeology* 34 (1981): 34–43.

24. As Pellicori states it at "Shroud," p. 42, the baking of the cloth was intended "to reproduce the effects of slow extended aging."

25. Schwalbe and Rogers, "Physics," p. 33.

26. Ibid., p. 30.

27. Joe Nickell, "The Shroud of Turin—Unmasked," *The Humanist* 38 (1978): 20.

28. Nickell, *Inquest*, pp. 101–3 and 135 ff.

29. Schwalbe and Rogers, "Physics," p. 30.

Chapter III: The Identity of the Man of the Shroud

1. Memorandum of Pierre d'Arcis, Bishop of Troyes, to Pope Clement VII. This memorandum was translated into English by Herbert Thurston in "The Holy Shroud and the Verdict of History," pp. 17–29, and that translation is presented by Wilson as Appendix B, *Shroud*, pp. 266–72. I follow the Thurston translation here.

2. For documented discussion of this important figure in the Shroud's history, see Wilson, *Shroud*, pp. 89–92.

3. Schwalbe and Rogers, "Physics," p. 40.

4. Barbet, *Doctor at Calvary*, 1963 reprint.

5. V. Tzaferis, "Jewish Tombs at and near Giv'at ha-Mivtar, Jerusalem," *Israel Exploration Journal* 20 (1970): 18–32.

6. N. Haas, "Skeletal Remains from Giv'at ha-Mivtar," *Israel Exploration Journal* 20 (1970): 38–59.

7. Wilson, *Shroud*, pp. 32–45 ("The Shroud and Medical Opinion") presents the conclusions of Delage, Barbet, Bucklin, and other specialists in some detail.

8. Stevenson and Habermas, *Verdict on the Shroud*, pp. 163–67.

9. For discussion of this point see Frederik van der Meer, *Early Christian Art*, trans. Peter and Friedl Brown (Chicago: University of Chicago Press, 1967), pp. 120–22. Cf. also W. F. Volbach and Max Hirmer, *Early Christian Art* (New York: Harry N. Abrams, n.d.), p. 22: "The death of Christ is alluded to by other scenes, but it is never actually portrayed. Old Testament scenes, such as the Sacrifice of Isaac or the representation of the Washing of the Hands, were enough for the believers."

10. For the Santa Sabina reliefs see Volbach and Hirmer, ibid., plate 103 (the panel in the upper left-hand corner very awkwardly depicts the crucifixion; the three crucified men are shown with their upper arms at their sides, and their lower arms extended horizontally). Another crucifixion scene possibly from the fifth century appears on an ivory casket: see Volbach and Hirmer, plate 98. On the Rabbula Codex illumination see van der Meer, *Early Christian Art*, plate 45 and p. 122: "And when the artists dared, at last, to represent Christ Himself on the Cross, He is clad in a long robe and stretches out his arms 'the whole day long, towards a stiff-necked people.' "

Chapter IV: The Mandylion

1. Wilson, *Shroud*. The key discussion runs from p. 84 to p. 124.

2. The story is discussed, and its evolution traced, by von Dobschuetz in Chapter 5 ("Das Christusbild von Edessa"—pp. 102–96) of *Christusbilder*. Perhaps a few explanatory remarks about this valuable book are appropriate here. After the 294 pages of analysis that make up the first part of *Christusbilder*, von Dobschuetz presented on 335 asterisked pages the *Belegen* ("documents") on which his analysis was based: here one finds the shorter and straightforward ancient and medieval texts, topically and chronologically arranged. Finally, in 357 pages with double asterisks von Dobschuetz presented a series of *Beilagen* ("appendices"); in this section appear the longer or problematical texts, together with von Dobschuetz's discussion of textual problems. The whole book is a remarkable scholarly achievement. Unfortunately, it has long been out of print, and the 1899 printing was done on paper of poor quality.

3. Vignon, *Le Saint Suaire de Turin*; Wuenschel, *Self-Portrait of Christ*; Maurus Green, "Enshrouded in Silence," *Ampleforth Journal* 74 (1969): 319–45; Wilson, *Shroud*, pp. 104–5.

4. Wilson, *Shroud*, pp. 120 ff.

5. This text, which Wilson calls "Story of the Image of Edessa" but which I shall refer to as the "Festival Sermon," appears in *Christusbilder* as Text B in "Beilage II" (pp. 39**–85**, odd-numbered pages only). The English translation followed here, prepared by Bernard Slater and the boys of Bradford Grammar School, in West Yorkshire, England, is presented by Wilson, *Shroud*, Appendix C (pp. 272–90). The Greek text can also be found in Migne, *Patrologia Graeca*, Vol. 113, cols. 423–54. The section numbering adopted by Wilson, and which I follow here, corresponds to the Roman numerals in von Dobschuetz's edition.

6. Wilson, *Shroud*, p. 120. For the Greek text see von Dobschuetz, Document 24 (Kap. V), p. 182*. For the English translation of the *Acts of Thaddaeus*, see A. Roberts and J. Donaldson, eds., *The Ante-Nicene Fathers*, Vol. 8 (New York:

Scribners, 1926), pp. 558–59. On the uniqueness of the word *tetradiplon,* see Wilson, *Shroud,* p. 307, n. 16.

7. Stevenson and Habermas, *Verdict on the Shroud,* pp. 30–31.

8. Von Dobschuetz found the Greek text of what he called "The Liturgical Tractate" appended to two codices of the "Festival Sermon." He presented the text in *Christusbilder,* "Beilage II, C" (pp. 110**–114**). In citing this text I follow von Dobschuetz's numbering of the paragraphs.

9. "Liturgical Tractate," 2.

10. "Monthly Lection," 25 (*Christusbilder,* p. 80**). For this text see below, note 19.

11. "Liturgical Tractate," 4.

12. According to Steven Runciman, "Some Remarks on the Image of Edessa," *Cambridge Hisorical Journal* 3 (1929–31): 248, in the tenth century *mandylion* "was a word long engrained in the Arabic language" but "was new as a Greek word." Cf., however, J. B. Segal, *Edessa, 'The Blessed City'* (Oxford: Clarendon Press, 1970), p. 215, n. 1.

13. For the "Life of St. Paul of Latros" see *Christusbilder,* Document 70 (Kap. V), p. 216*. Other instances of the word *mandylion* in Greek texts appear in Documents 57* and 78g–85d in the same series. The word is also used in Document 110, but that text, a handbook on painting composed at Mt. Athos, dates from ca. 1600.

14. For an index of the terms used to describe the Edessan Icon, or the Mandylion, see ibid., pp. 248*–49*.

15. Ibid., Document 71 (Kap. V), p. 217*.

16. Ibid., Document 30b (Kap. V), p. 189*.

17. Ibid., "Beilage III," pp. 130**–35**.

18. Ibid., Documents 105 and 109 (Kap. V), pp. 243* and 247*.

19. After collating six manuscripts of the Menologium, von Dobschuetz presented the Greek text ("Die Menaeenlektion zum Fest der Translation am 16. Aug.") in *Christusbilder,* "Beilage II A," pp. 38**–84** (even-numbered pages only). I follow his paragraph enumeration. The key passage is at para. 5 (p. 48**).

20. See Averil Cameron, *The Sceptic and the Shroud. An Inaugural Lecture in the Departments of Classics and History delivered at King's College London on 29th April 1980* (London[?], 1980[?]), for an argument against Wilson's identification of the Shroud with the Mandylion. Cameron's procedure is to beg the question that Wilson set out to answer. See her statement on pp. 8–9: "In any case, the form of the Image of Edessa story . . . makes quite impossible the notion that the cloth in question could have been the extant shroud, even if we could believe the idea that it was folded (why?) for many centuries in such a way that only the face could be seen. For Christ wiped his *face* on the cloth while he was alive and gave the cloth himself to Abgar's messenger; this is utterly different from what is suggested by the Shroud, which bears beyond all doubt the complete bodily image back and front of a dead and wounded man lying in a prone position, and could only have acquired its markings from a body lying in such a way." Wilson's point was that just as we cannot take the Edessan and Byzantine authors' word for the way in which their cloth was imprinted, so we must not take them at their word that the cloth portrayed only a face.

Cameron proposes that the Edessans constructed a series of artifacts—first a portrait painted on a plaque, then a figured cloth—to keep up with the evolving legend. See *Sceptic,* p. 9: "there must have been a moment when a physical picture—and later a cloth with an imprinted face—must actually have been produced in response to the desire to validate the growing story." In other words, the Edessan Icon was first made of wood, but then the Edessans began describing it as a cloth, and therefore were obliged to replace their wooden icon with a cloth icon.

21. Wilson, *Shroud*, pp. 102–6, 114–15, and 173.

22. André Grabar, *La Sainte Face de Laon. Le Mandylion dans l'art orthodoxe* (Prague: Seminarium Kondakovianum, 1931), p. 20.

23. The Old Church Slavonic inscription, *obraz gospodni naübrüse*, remained unintelligible until the eighteenth century; for the amusing translations that had before that time been suggested see Grabar, *Sainte Face*, pp. 11–13.

24. Grabar, *Sainte Face*, pp. 16–18.

25. Wilson, *Shroud*, pp. 157–64.

26. Ibid., p. 160.

27. Translation from ibid., p. 169. For the text see *Christusbilder*, p. 146*: "li Sydoines, là où Nostre Sires fut envolepés, i estoit, qui cascuns devenres se drechoit tous drois, si que on i pooit bien veïr le figure Notre Seigneur."

28. *Christusbilder*, Document 91 (Kap. V), p. 232*.

29. "Liturgical Tractate," 4.

30. Ibid.

31. "Latin Abgar Legend," 4 (*Christusbilder*, "Beilage III," p. 133**).

32. Ibid., 6–7 (*Christusbilder*, p. 134**).

33. *Christusbilder*, pp. 139**, and 194*, at Document 40 (Kap. V).

34. Ibid., Document 81 (Kap. V), p. 224*.

35. Von Dobschuetz printed this text as a footnote, *Christusbilder*, pp. 133**–34**.

36. Gervase of Tilbury, *Otia Imperialia* 3. 24 (ed. Leibnitz). Von Dobschuetz presents excerpts from this text at *Christusbilder*, pp. 290**–91**, n. 5. For the full text and discussion see Savio, *Ricerche storica sulla Santa Sindone*, p. 358, n. 74. The same story appears in a text perhaps dating ca. 1300, the *Relatio Leobini*. For this text see Savio, *Ricerche*, pp. 356–57 and 380.

37. Wilson, *Shroud*, pp. 169–72.

38. Ibid., pp. 172–91. For criticism of Wilson's reconstruction see Malcolm Barber, "The Templars and the Turin Shroud," *Shroud Spectrum International* 2 (1983): 16–34.

39. Runciman, "Remarks," p. 251.

40. P. de Riant, *Exuviae Sacrae Constantinopolitanae*, Vol. 2 (Geneva, 1878), pp. 135 ff. Von Dobschuetz read the line *sanctam toellam tabulae insertam* (*Christusbilder*, Document 96 [Kap. V], p. 237*). Cf. Runciman, "Remarks," p. 251.

41. *Christusbilder*, pp. 186–87.

Chapter V: The Edessan Icon

1. The best history of the city is Segal's *Edessa, 'The Blessed City'.*

2. These appear in the anonymous *Acts of Thaddaeus* (*Christusbilder*, Document 24 [Kap. V], p. 182*), and in Evagrius's *Ecclesiastical History* (see below, note 14).

3. For the eighth-century references, see *Christusbilder*, Documents 26–30, 33, and 35–42 (Kap. V), pp. 183*–96*. A possible seventh-century allusion to the icon appears in a hymn discovered after von Dobschuetz' collection was published. See André Grabar, "Le témoignage d'une hymne syriaque sur l'ar-

chitecture de la cathédrale d'Edesse au VIᵉ siècle et sur la symbolique de l'édifice chrétien," in his collection of essays, *L'Art de la fin de l'antiquité et du Moyen Age*, Vol. 1 (1968), pp. 39 and 43.

4. *Christusbilder*, Document 6 (Kap. V), p. 171*.

5. A. A. Vasiliev, *History of the Byzantine Empire*, Vol. 1 (Madison: University of Wisconsin Press, 1958), p. 230.

6. Runciman, "Some Remarks on the Image of Edessa," pp. 238–52; Wilson, *Shroud*, pp. 126 ff.

7. See Chapter IV, note 5.

8. Runciman, "Remarks," p. 244, suggested that "in the stress of the siege, possibly in the course of the mining work, an old icon fell into the hands of the orthodox clergy," and supposed that the cloth had been "somewhere hidden in a wall or a cellar."

9. Wilson, *Shroud*, p. 138.

10. Procopius, *On Buildings* 2. 7.

11. Wilson, *Shroud*, p. 139.

12. For a Latin translation (by I. Guidi) of this Syriac text, see *Chronica Minora* II (Louvain, 1955), which is also Vol. 2 of the *Scriptores Syri* section of the massive *Corpus Scriptorum Christianorum Orientalium*.

13. "Edessan Chronicle" Entries XC and XCI: "In the 836th year [i.e., A.D. 525], a deluge for the fourth time overwhelmed Edessa. It undermined the walls, overturned the buildings of the city, and drowned the citizens, involving widespread ruin of the entire city. For this reason Bishop Asclepius fled from Edessa and went straight to Antioch, to the Patriarch Euphrasius: and there, at Antioch, about seventy days later, he died on the 27th of June of that year, and was buried right there, at Antioch. On the 4th of September of that year his corpse was fetched from Antioch and was buried in the Church of St. Barlaha, next to the bishop, St. Nonnus."

14. Evagrius, *Historiae Ecclesiasticae* Libri VI-Vol. 86, 2 in Migne, *Patrologia Graeca*.

15. Evagrius, *Eccl. Hist.* 4. 27. In *Christusbilder* this passage appears in "Beilage II," pp. 68** and 70**.

16. "Geschichte des Dominus Mâri," *Christusbilder*, Document 41 (Kap. V), p. 195*.

17. Ibid., Document 48 (Kap. V), p. 200*.

18. Ps.-John of Damascus; *Christusbilder*, Document 30c (Kap. V), pp. 189* –90*.

19. John of Damascus; *Christusbilder*, Document 30a (Kap. V), p. 189*.

20. Segal, *Edessa*, pp. 87–93 and 170–73.

21. G.E. Gingras, trans., *Egeria: Diary of a Pilgrimage*. Ancient Christian Writers , no. 38 (New York: Newman Press, 1970). See chap. 19.

22. Eusebius, *History of the Church* 1. 13.

23. This text has recently been republished, along with an English translation: George Howard, trans., *The Teaching of Addai* (Chico, Calif.: Scholars Press, 1981). On the date of the manuscripts, see Howard's introductory remarks, p. viii.

24. Howard's translation of sec. 3b-4a (for an older translation see *Christusbilder*, Document 6 [Kap. V], p. 171*).

25. *Christusbilder*, pp. 105–13.

26. Procopius, *de Bello Persico* 2. 26–27.

27. Ibid., 2. 12.

28. Evagrius, *Eccl. Hist.* 4. 26 and 4. 28. The story of Edessa's deliverance by the icon (4. 27) is sandwiched between these two stories of the miraculous deliverance of Apamea and Sergiopolis from the army of Chosroes.

29. Ukhthanes of Urha and Stephanus of Tarôn, both of whom lived ca. 1000, repeat the interpretation of Moses of Khorene. See *Christusbilder*, Documents 26, 69 and 73 (Kap. V), pp. 184*, 215*, and 219*.

30. Edward Gibbon, *The History of the Decline and Fall of the Roman Empire*, chap. 49 (p. 876 in the London [Ball, Arnold and Co.] ed., 1840).

31. Segal, *Edessa*, pp. 77 and 213–14.

32. See von Dobschuetz's comments at *Christusbilder*, Document 4 (Kap. V), pp. 165*–67*.

33. See note 21.

34. Wilson, *Shroud*, pp. 135–38; Wilson's demythologized version of the story is accepted at face value by Stevenson and Habermas, *Verdict on the Shroud*, p. 22.

35. *Doctrine of Addai* 4a: "When King Abgar saw the portrait he received it with great joy and placed it with great honor in one of the buildings of his palaces" (Howard's translation).

36. "Festival Sermon," 16.

37. The story appears in a Greek text, probably composed in the eighth century, celebrating the Caesarean icon's festival day. The text is presented in *Christusbilder*, "Beilage I," pp. 12**–18**.

38. Ibid., pp. 57 and 24**–25**.

39. Ibid., p. 9**.

40. Ibid., p. 119.

41. Eusebius, *History of the Church* 1. 13. 5–10. A late third-century Syriac story of the acts of Thaddaeus/Addai is generally assumed as Eusebius's source. See von Dobschuetz, *Christusbilder*, pp. 164*–65* and 171*; Runciman, "Remarks," p. 241; Segal, *Edessa*, p. 62, n. 3.

42. The few verbal differences are noted by Segal, *Edessa*, pp. 62–63.

43. Runciman, "Remarks," pp. 241–42.

44. The text is very explicit about this: "Receiving Ananias, and falling down before the icon and worshipping it, Abgar was healed of his disease before Thaddaeus ever got there" (*Acta Thaddaei* 4).

45. Syrian Christians believed that Addai was the evangelist who brought Christianity to Edessa. Greek Christians knew nothing about an Addai, and identified him as Thaddaeus, a name at least mentioned in the New Testament. A Thaddaeus appears as one of the Twelve in some manuscripts of Matthew 10 : 3 (other manuscripts read Lebbaeus), and at Mark 3 : 18. In the lists at Luke 6 : 16 and Acts 1 : 13 there is neither a Thaddaeus nor a Lebbaeus, but a Judas, son of James. Christian scholars of late antiquity concluded that Thaddaeus and Judas were alternate names for the same person, and we occasionally hear that the evangelist of Edessa was Judas. Eusebius (*Hist. of the Church* 1. 13), on the other hand, had identified the Edessans' Thaddaeus not as one of the Twelve, but as one of the Seventy. See Segal, *Edessa*, p. 66. At any rate, the earliest writer in *Christusbilder* who credits Thaddaeus with bringing the cloth to Edessa was the patriarch Germanus, in 729; that version next appears in 836 (*Christusbilder*, Documents 29 and 48 [Kap. V], pp. 188* and 200*).

46. Segal, *Edessa*, p. 70.

47. Ibid., pp. 50–61.

48. Eusebius, *History of the Church* 5. 22.

Chapter VI: The Forma Christi

1. The exceptions to this rule are admirably presented by Cecil Roth, ed., *Jewish Art, An Illustrated History*, 2nd ed. (New York: New York Graphic Society, 1971).

2. In the nineteenth century there was a lively debate about the absence or presence of representational art in earliest Christianity, with some Catholic historians arguing that from the very beginning of the Church images had had their rightful place. The fullest study of the matter was Hugo Koch's *Die altchristliche Bilderfrage nach den literarischen Quellen* (Göttingen: Vandenhoeck & Ruprecht, 1917), which more or less settled the question. The present view is concisely stated by André Grabar, *Christian Iconography: A Study of Its Origins* (London: Routledge & Kegan Paul, 1969), p. 7: "The earliest Christian images appeared somewhere about the year 200. This means that during roughly a century and a half the Christians did without any figurative representations of a religious character."

3. Epiphanius, *Letter to John of Jerusalem*; Eusebius, *Letter to Empress Constantia* (*Christusbilder*, Documents 5 and 6 [Kap. II], pp. 101*–2*).

4. For the paintings at Dura-Europus, both those of the Christian house and the more spectacular painting of the Jewish synagogue, see André Grabar, *The Beginnings of Christian Art, 200–395*, trans. Stuart Gilbert and James Emmons from the French (London: Thames & Hudson, 1967), pp. 59–80, and figs. 52–53 and 59–71.

5. Cf. Eusebius, for example, in his letter responding to the Empress Constantia's request for an image of Jesus: "You have not forgotten, have you, that God commands us to make no likeness, whether of things in heaven above or in earth beneath? Have you yourself ever heard, or have you ever heard from someone else, of such things in the Church? . . . Such things are not permissible for us" (Eusebius, *Epistola ad Constantiam Augustam;* Migne, *Pat. Graeca*, vol. 20, col. 1548C.

6. For a survey of this third- and fourth-century art see Grabar, *Beginnings,* and Pierre du Bourguet, *Early Christian Art,* trans. Thomas Burton from the French (New York: Reynal & Co., in association with Wm. Morrow, 1971).

7. Augustine, *De Trinitate*, 8.4.7.

8. Origen, *Contra Celsum*, 6.75, trans. Henry Chadwick (Cambridge: Cambridge University Press, 1953).

9. See, for instance, J. Burns, *The Christ Face in Art* (London: Duckworth, 1907), or Denis Thomas, *The Face of Christ* (New York: Doubleday, 1979). Von Dobschuetz (*Christusbilder*, p. 30) concluded that it was impossible that what eventually became the conventional image of Christ "auf eine gute geschichtliche Überlieferung zurückgehe."

10. Wilson, *Shroud*, pp. 100–102, argued that the "familiar" Christ likeness appeared only after 525, the date at which Wilson supposed that the Shroud was rediscovered atop Edessa's main gate. But by 525 the "familiar" likeness had already appeared frequently, and at least in the Eastern Empire was well on its way to displacing the Classical Youth as the conventional representation of Christ. Cf. van der Meer, *Early Christian Art*, p. 102: "In the Greek East . . . the figure of the youthful, timeless teacher was replaced by the face we all know, whose origin is still obscure—the young, bearded man, his hair parted in the middle and falling to his shoulders, with a finely-wrought, narrow, straight

nose, an expressive but narrow tight-closed mouth. . . . The figure of the Shepherd, and the other symbolic representations, vanished almost completely after 400."

11. Irenaeus, *Adversus Haereses*, 1.25.6.

12. On the success of the Christians' persecution of Gnosticism, see Elaine Pagels, *The Gnostic Gospels* (New York: Random House, 1979), p. xxiv. For Hegesippus's account of Gnostic origins, see Eusebius, *History of the Church* 4. 22.

13. Translations of all the Nag Hammadi texts are now available in the single volume edited by James M. Robinson, *The Nag Hammadi Library* (New York: Harper & Row, 1981).

14. For the one view, cf. R. Schnackenburg, "Early Gnosticism," in *Jesus in His Time*, ed. H. J. Schultz, trans. Brian Watchorn (Philadelphia: Fortress Press, 1971), p. 137: "All the indications . . . suggest that the new attitude to life which is to be designated gnostic may have arisen in the medley of religions and peoples in the area of Syria and Palestine not long before the emergence of Christianity but independently of it." R. M. Grant set forth the other view in *Gnosticism and Early Christianity*, 2nd ed. (New York: Harper, 1966).

On Simon Magus and the disciples of John the Baptist, see Grant, *Gnosticism*, p. 90. It is also pertinent that the Gnostic Mandaeans of southern Iraq and southwestern Iran trace their beginnings to John the Baptist; see F. E. Peters, *The Harvest of Hellenism* (New York: Simon & Schuster, 1970), pp. 639 and 668–69. On the Gnostic tendencies in the Qumran scrolls, see Robinson, *Nag Hammadi*, p. 7. Although many scholars have spoken readily about "pre-Christian Gnosticism," others have recently challenged the term. See, for example, Edwin M. Yamauchi, *Pre-Christian Gnosticism: A Survey of the Proposed Evidences* (Grand Rapids, Mich.: Wm. B. Eerdmans Publishing Co., 1973). On pp. 184–85 Yamauchi summarizes: "The imposing edifice of Reitzenstein's and Bultmann's pre-Christian Gnosticism is but little more than an elaborate multi-storied, many-roomed house of cards."

15. Grant, *Gnosticism*, p. 10.

16. Schnackenburg, "Early Gnosticism," pp. 138–39.

17. See Bentley Layton, *The Gnostic Treatise on Resurrection from Nag Hammadi* (Missoula, Mont.: Scholars Press, 1979), p. 1: "To no small degree the historical importance of the treatise lies in its detailed and sympathetic exposition of a celebrated heresy attacked by the author of the Pastoral Epistles (2 Tim. 2 : 17), *resurrectionem esse iam factam.*"

18. On the tomb, see Ernest Nash, *Pictorial Dictionary of Ancient Rome*, vol. 2 (New York: Praeger, 1962), pp. 311–19, and illustrations 1075–1084. For a color plate of the painting important for our purposes, see Du Bourguet, *Early Christian Art*, p. 41, or Grabar, *Beginnings of Christian Art*, ill. 107 (p. 109).

19. Grabar, *Beginnings of Christian Art*, p. 108.

20. Ibid., p. 110. For a full discussion of the para-Christian art in this tomb, see J. Stevenson, *The Catacombs* (London: Thames & Hudson, 1978), pp. 111–17.

21. Painting of bust of Christ in Catacomb of Commodilla: Du Bourguet, *Early Christian Art*, p. 123, and Grabar, *Beginnings*, ill. 237. The two S. Costanza mosaics: Du Bourguet, *Art*, pp. 129 and 131; Grabar, *Beginnings*, ill. 207, p. 192; and Grabar, *Christian Iconography*, ill. 101. Other fourth-century Roman examples of the long-haired, bearded Christ include a magnificent ceiling painting of Christ between Peter and Paul, in the Crypt of the Saints at the Catacomb of Saints Peter and Marcellinus (Du Bourguet, *Art*, p. 171; Grabar, *Beginnings*, ill. 233 and 234), and a relief of Christ among the Disciples, on the Borghese

Sarcophagus, now in the Louvre (Du Bourguet, *Art*, p. 158). Grabar, *Iconography*, p. 71, reports yet another late fourth- or early fifth-century example in a recently discovered and unpublished marquetry at Ostia: "Physically, the head of Christ in the marquetry at Ostia (the long hair, rather abundant beard, and the general expression) is close to the mosaic of S. Pudenziana and to one in a fresco in the catacomb of Commodilla." The Santa Pudenziana mosaic dates from the early fifth century.

22. For a general discussion of Gnosticism in Edessa see Segal, *Edessa*, pp. 43–45.

23. Edited and translated by D. Parrott and W. Schoedel, in Robinson, *Nag Hammadi Library*, pp. 242–48.

24. The fullest treatment of this enigmatic figure is H. J. W. Drijvers, *Bardaiṣan of Edessa* (Assen: van Gorcum, 1966).

25. Julian, *Letters* 424C–425A.

26. Walter Bauer, *Rechtgläubigkeit und Ketzerei im ältesten Christentum*, 2nd ed. (Tübingen: Mohr, 1964). The first edition of this important book was published in 1934. An English translation is also available: *Orthodoxy and Heresy in Earliest Christianity* (Philadelphia: Fortress Press, 1971).

27. In her *Gnostic Gospels*, pp. 102–18 (a chapter entitled "Whose Church Is the 'True Church'?"), Elaine Pagels shows that the Nag Hammadi texts tend to corroborate Bauer's conclusions.

28. Grant, *Gnosticism*, pp. 155–77.

29. Morton Smith, *Clement of Alexandria and a Secret Gospel of Mark* (Cambridge, Mass.: Harvard University Press, 1973).

30. For the Greek text and Smith's translation of the fragment see Smith, *Clement*, pp. 446–52.

31. Irenaeus, *Adversus Haereses* 1.25.6 (von Dobschuetz, *Christusbilder*, Document 1a (Kap. II), p. 98*).

32. Epiphanius, *Against Heresies* 27.6 (Migne, *Pat. Graeca*, vol. 41, col. 374C; von Dobschuetz, *Christusbilder*, Document 1b (Kap. II), p. 98*).

33. Hippolytus, *Refut.* 7.32 (*Christusbilder*, Document 1c (Kap. II), p. 98*). The reference to Simon's and Carpocras's icon of Christ appears in Photius, *Amphilochia* 194; see *Christusbilder*, Document 1f (Kap. II), p. 99*.

34. "Monthly Lection," 19 and 21; "Festival Sermon," 2, 17 and 21 (*ektypōsis*). For references to the imprint on the Sacred Tile as an *ektypōma*, see *Christusbilder*, Documents 71, 78d, 80b and 85b (Kap. V).

35. Although Epiphanius's and Hippolytus's paraphrases suggest that Pilate made more than one image of Christ, the Latin translation of *Against Heresies* indicates that Irenaeus himself had used the singular. The ambiguity may be fortuitous, but it is conceivable that it arose from inconsistent reports of the Shroud's image or images (i.e., frontal and dorsal).

36. Antoninus Placentinus, *Itinerarium* 23 (*Christusbilder*, Document 2 (Kap. II), p. 99*).

Chapter VII: The Sindon

1. Donna Kurtz and John Boardman, *Greek Burial Customs* (Ithaca: Cornell University Press, 1971), especially pp. 144 and 207, and plates 33, 34 and 35; Jocelyn Toynbee, *Death and Burial in the Roman World* (Ithaca: Cornell University Press, 1971), p. 44.

2. Humber, *Sacred Shroud*, p. 63: "Even the most ascetic rabbis who were buried in simple sheets probably wore the sheets draped around their bodies, as they had done in life. Whether in splendor or in simplicity, Jews were buried in clothing rather than in shrouds. The handkerchief over the face was at first optional and later mandatory, but the main garment was never draped over the head." Humber, like many other sindonologists, concludes that the Shroud was not a shroud at all, but a temporary covering for Jesus' body, which was given only a "provisional" burial on Good Friday. For a full description of ancient Jewish beliefs and practices concerning the clothing of a corpse, see A. P. Bender, "Beliefs, Rites and Customs of the Jews, Connected with Death, Burial and Mourning, V," *Jewish Quarterly Review* 7 (1894–95): 261–64.

3. E. A. W. Budge, *The Mummy. Chapters on Egyptian Funereal Archaeology*, 2nd ed. (New York: Biblo and Tannen, 1964 reprint), p. 191.

4. For Wilson's statement, see *Shroud*, p. 246. For Jackson's statements and a full account of the results of the test on the VP-8 Image Analyzer, see John Jackson, Eric Jumper, Bill Mottern, and Kenneth Stevenson, "The Three Dimensional Image on Jesus' Burial Cloth," *Proceedings of the 1977 United States Conference of Research on the Shroud of Turin* (New York: Holy Shroud Guild, 1977), pp. 74 and 82.

5. Wilson, *Shroud*, p. 246.

6. *The Holy Shroud* (New York: Holy Shroud Guild, 1954). For the same explanation, see Father Wuenschel's *Self-Portrait of Christ*, p. 21. For a different explanation of the parallel bands, see Schwalbe and Rogers, "Physics," p. 24: the "abrupt change in the image density" at the side of the face, they suggest, "might be observed from a block print or rubbing where thread-lot thickness or surface discontinuities affected the amount of material transferred in the process. In this particular region, the radiographs show no discontinuity in the cloth areal density; it can therefore be concluded that adjacent warp thread-lots differed either in their surface or chemical charactristics." See also their comments at Fig. 4, p. 19.

7. We have already noticed in Chapter V a seventh- or eighth-century story that supposed that the cloth of Camulia and the cloth of Caesarea were one and the same. An earlier, and less confused, story is presented at *Christusbilder*, "Beilage I," pp. 4**–7**. According to this Syriac text, a woman named Hypatia (who was not yet a Christian) one day discovered, in a fountain in her garden, a cloth bearing the image of Jesus. To her amazement, the cloth was entirely dry when she removed it from the fountain. She wrapped it in her mantle, and when later she unwrapped it, she found that the image had miraculously copied itself on the mantle. For the one cloth Hypatia built a sanctuary at Camulia, and the other was taken to Caesarea. The same text reports that another miraculous copy of the Camulian Icon was displayed at Diobulion, where the people called it an *acheiropoietos* icon.

8. For the creation of the Melitene Icon, see *Christusbilder*, Document 4 (Kap. III), pp. 125*–127*. In the reign of Tiberius II (578–82) the Camulian Icon, which by that time had been brought to Constantinople, was loaned to a patrician lady named Maria, who had a terrible disease and who hoped that the Camulian Icon would heal her. Not only did it heal her, but it miraculously copied itself on one of her silks that was exactly the same size as the original cloth. Maria gave the silk to a nuns' cloister in Melitene, but when that city was attacked by the Persians in the reign of Heraclius (610–41), the cloth was brought to Constantinople.

9. Antoninus Placentinus, *Itinerarium* 44. The text is given in *Christusbilder* as Document 1 (Kap. IV), p. 135*.

10. To these probable parallels to the Shroud in the sixth century, one might also add the Shroud of Besançon. Although it is possible that the image on the Besançon cloth was painted, and that it was inspired by the exhibition of our Shroud at Lirey in the 1350s (see Wilson, *Shroud*, p. 212), it is also possible that the Besançon cloth too held an ancient imprint. Von Dobschuetz, *Christusbilder*, p. 74, suggested that the cloth had come to Besançon before 1349, the year in which a fire destroyed the church's archives. The story was that the Besançon Shroud had been brought to France by a Crusader, but we cannot know whether the story was based on fact.

11. John 19 : 40 and 20 : 7.

12. Jerome, *De Viris Illustribus*, chap. 2, 831–33=Migne, *Patrologia Latina*, Vol. 23, cols. 611–13. For the other surviving fragments of the *Gospel according to the Hebrews*, and for a discussion of the date (early second century) and character of the gospel, see P. Vielhauer, "The Jewish Christian Gospels," in *New Testament Apocrypha*, vol. I, ed. E. Hennecke (Philadelphia: Westminster Press, 1963), pp. 158–65.

13. For the story that Simon Magus carried about with him an image of Christ, see Chapter VI, note 33.

14. James M. Robinson, "Jesus: From Easter to Valentinus," *Journal of Biblical Literature* 101 (1982): 5–37.

15. Wayne Meeks, *The First Urban Christians* (New Haven: Yale University Press, 1983), p. 182. Although Paul, like some Gnostics, tried to differentiate between a "spiritual" and an "animate" body, the distinction was difficult to grasp, and Paul's presentation seems to have contributed greatly to the belief that Jesus' corpse had come back to life. For an analysis of Paul's views on resurrection, see Michael Grant, *Saint Paul* (New York: Charles Scribners, 1976), p. 80.

Bibliography

Ashe, Geoffrey. "What Sort of Picture?" *Sindon* (1966): 15–19. (*Sindon* is a journal published by the Centro Internazionale di Sindonologia, in Turin.)

Barber, Malcolm. "The Templars and the Turin Shroud." *Shroud Spectrum International* 2 (1983): 16–34. (*Shroud Spectrum International* is a journal published by the Indiana Center for Shroud Studies, Box 557, Nashville, Ind. 47448.)

Barbet, Pierre. *Doctor at Calvary*. New York: P. J. Kenedy and Sons, 1953; reprint, Image Books, 1963.

Bauer, Walter. *Rechtgläubigkeit und Ketzerei im ältesten Christentum*. 2nd ed. Tübingen: Mohr, 1964. (Translated into English as *Orthodoxy and Heresy in Earliest Christianity*. Philadelphia: Fortress Press, 1971).

Bender, A. P. "Beliefs, Rites and Customs of the Jews, Connected with Death, Burial and Mourning, V." *Jewish Quarterly Review* 7 (1894–95): 259–69.

Bourguet, Pierre du. *Early Christian Art*. Translated from the French by Thomas Burton. New York: Reynal & Co., in association with Wm. Morrow, 1971.

Budge, E. A. W. *The Mummy. Chapters on Egyptian Funereal Archaeology*. 2nd ed. New York: Biblo and Tannen, 1964 reprint.

Burns, J. *The Christ Face in Art*. London: Duckworth, 1907.

Cameron, Averil. *The Sceptic and the Shroud. An Inaugural Lecture in the Departments of Classics and History Delivered at King's College London on 29th April 1980*. London(?), 1980(?).

Carter, Howard, and A. C. Mace. *The Tomb of Tutankhamen*. Vols. 2 and 3. New York: Cooper Square, 1963.

Chevalier, Ulysse. *Etude critique sur l'origine du Saint Suaire de Lirey-Chambery-Turin*. Paris: A. Picard, 1900.

Dobschuetz, Ernst von. *Christusbilder. Untersuchungen zur christlichen Legende*. Leipzig: J. C. Hinrichs'sche Buchhandlung, 1899.

Drijvers, H. J. W. *Bardaiṣan of Edessa*. Assen: van Gorcum, 1966.

Forbes, R. J. *Studies in Ancient Technology*, vol. 4. Leiden: Brill, 1964.

Gibbon, Edward. *The History of the Decline and Fall of the Roman Empire*. London: Ball, Arnold and Co., 1840.

Gingras, G. E., trans. *Egeria: Diary of a Pilgrimage*. Ancient Christian Writers, no. 38. New York: Newman Press, 1970.

Grabar, André. *La Sainte Face de Laon: Le Mandylion dans l'art orthodoxe*. Prague: Seminarium Kondakovianum, 1931.

——————. *The Beginnings of Christian Art, 200–395.* Translated from the French by Stuart Gilbert and James Emmons. London: Thames & Hudson, 1967.

——————. "Le temoignage d'une hymne syriaque sur l'architecture de la cathedrale d'Edesse au VIe siecle et sur la symbolique de l'edifice chretien." Pp. 31–50 in his *L'Art de la fin de l'Antiquite et du Moyen Âge,* vol. 1. Paris: College de France, 1968.

——————. *Christian Iconography: A Study of Its Origins.* London: Routledge & Kegan Paul, 1969.

Grant, Michael. *Saint Paul.* New York: Scribners, 1976.

Grant, R. M. *Gnosticism and Early Christianity.* 2nd ed. New York: Harper, 1966.

Green, Maurus. "Enshrouded in Silence." *Ampleforth Journal* 74 (1969): 319–45.

Haas, N. "Skeletal Remains from Giv'at ha-Mivtar." *Israel Exploration Journal* 20 (1970): 38–59.

Heller, J. H., and A. D. Adler. "A Chemical Investigation of the Shroud of Turin." *Canadian Society of Forensic Science Journal* 14 (1981): 81–103.

Heller, John H. *Report on the Shroud of Turin.* New York: Houghton Mifflin, 1983.

The Holy Shroud. New York: Holy Shroud Guild, 1954.

Howard, George, trans. *The Teaching of Addai.* Chico, Calif.: Scholars Press, 1981.

Humber, Thomas. *The Sacred Shroud.* New York: Pocket Books, 1977.

Jackson, John P., Eric Jumper, Bill Mottern, and Kenneth Stevenson. "The Three Dimensional Image on Jesus' Burial Cloth." *Proceedings of the 1977 United States Conference of Research on the Shroud of Turin.* New York: Holy Shroud Guild, 1977.

Koch, Hugo. *Die altchristliche Bilderfrage nach den literarischen Quellen.* Göttingen: Vandenhoeck & Ruprecht, 1917.

Kurtz, Donna, and John Boardman. *Greek Burial Customs.* Ithaca: Cornell University Press, 1971.

Layton, Bentley. *The Gnostic Treatise on Resurrection from Nag Hammadi.* Missoula, Mont.: Scholars Press, 1979.

Meeks, Wayne, *The First Urban Christians.* New Haven: Yale University Press, 1983.

Meer, Frederik van der. *Early Christian Art.* Translated by Peter and Friedl Brown. Chicago: University of Chicago Press, 1967.

Murphy, Cullen. "Shreds of Evidence." *Harper's* (November 1981): 42 ff.

Nash, Ernest. *Pictorial Dictionary of Ancient Rome.* New York: Praeger, 1962.

Nickell, Joe. "The Shroud of Turin—Unmasked." *The Humanist* 38 (1978): 20–22.

——————. *Inquest on the Shroud of Turin.* Buffalo: Prometheus Books, 1983.

Pagels, Elaine. *The Gnostic Gospels.* New York: Random House, 1979.

Pellicori, S. F., and M. S. Evans. "The Shroud of Turin Through the Microscope." *Archaeology* 34 (1981): 34–43.

Peters, F. E. *The Harvest of Hellenism.* New York: Simon & Schuster, 1970.

Popham, M., E. Touloupa, and H. Sackett. "The Hero of Lefkandi." *Antiquity* 56 (1982): 169–74.

Riant, Paul E. D. *Exuviae Sacrae Constantinopolitanae.* Vol. 2. Geneva, 1878.

Riefstahl, Elizabeth. *Thebes in the Time of Amunhotep III.* Norman: University of Oklahoma Press, 1964.

Rinaldi, Peter. "Turin and the Holy Shroud." *Proceedings of the 1977 United States Conference of Research on the Shroud of Turin.* New York: Holy Shroud Guild, 1977.

Robinson, James M., ed. *The Nag Hammadi Library.* New York: Harper & Row, 1981.

————. "Jesus: From Easter to Valentinus." *Journal of Biblical Literature* 101 (1982): 5–37.

Roth, Cecil, ed. *Jewish Art, An Illustrated History.* 2nd ed. New York: New York Graphic Society, 1971.

Runciman, Steven. "Some Remarks on the Image of Edessa." *Cambridge Historical Journal* 3 (1929–1931): 238–52.

Savio, Pietro. *Ricerche storiche sulla Santa Sindone.* Turin: Società Editrice Internazionale, 1957.

Schnackenburg, R. "Early Gnosticism." Pp. 132–41 in H. J. Schultz, ed., *Jesus in His Time.* Translated from the German by Brian Watchorn. Philadelphia: Fortress Press, 1971.

Schwalbe, L. A., and R. N. Rogers. "Physics and Chemistry of the Shroud of Turin: A Summary of the 1978 Investigation." *Analytica Chimica Acta* 135 (1982): 3–49.

Segal, J.B. *Edessa, 'The Blessed City'.* Oxford: Clarendon Press, 1970.

La S. Sindone: Ricerche e studi della commissione di esperti nominata dall'Archivescovo di Torino, Card. Michele Pellegrino, nel 1969. Turin: 1976. Special issue of the *Rivista diocesana torinese.* For the English translation of this report, see entry *Turin Commission on the Holy Shroud, Report of the.*

Smith, Morton. *Clement of Alexandria and a Secret Gospel of Mark.* Cambridge, Mass.: Harvard University Press, 1973.

Stevenson, J. *The Catacombs.* London: Thames & Hudson, 1978.

Stevenson, Kenneth E., and Gary R. Habermas. *Verdict on the Shroud.* Wayne, Penna.: Dell/Banbury, 1981.

Thomas, Denis. *The Face of Christ.* New York: Doubleday, 1979.

Thurston, Herbert. "The Holy Shroud and the Verdict of History." *The Month* 101 (1903): 17–29.

————. "The Holy Shroud as a Scientific Problem." *The Month* 101 (1903): 162–78.

Toynbee, Jocelyn. *Death and Burial in the Roman World.* Ithaca: Cornell University Press, 1971.

Turin Commission on the Holy Shroud, Report of the. London: Screenpro Films (5 Meard St., London W1V 3HQ), 1976.

Tyrer, John. "Looking at the Shroud as a Textile." *Shroud Spectrum International* 2 (1983): 35–45.

Tzaferis, T. "Jewish Tombs at and near Giv'at ha-Mivtar, Jerusalem." *Israel Exploration Journal* 20 (1970): 18–32.

Vasiliev, A. A. *History of the Byzantine Empire.* Vol. 1. Madison: University of Wisconsin Press, 1958.

Vielhauer, P. "The Jewish Christian Gospels." Pp. 158–65 in E. Hennecke, ed., *New Testament Apocrypha.* Philadelphia: Westminster Press, 1963.

Vignon, Paul. *Le Saint Suaire de Turin devant la science, l'archéologie, l'histoire, l'iconographie, la logique.* 2nd ed. Paris: Masson, 1939.

Volbach, W. F., and Max Hirmer. *Early Christian Art.* New York: Harry N. Abrams, n.d.

Walsh, John. *The Shroud.* New York: Random House, 1963.

Wilcox, Robert. *Shroud.* New York: Macmillan, 1977.

Wilson, Ian. *The Shroud of Turin*. Rev. ed. New York: Image Books, 1979.
Wuenschel, Edward A. *Self-Portrait of Christ: The Holy Shroud of Turin*. Esopus,
    N.Y.: Holy Shroud Guild, 1957.
Yamauchi, Edwin M. *Pre-Christian Gnosticism: A Survey of the Proposed Evidences*.
    Grand Rapids, Mich.: Wm. B. Eerdmans, 1973.

Index